TWAYNE'S WORLD AUTHORS SERIES

A Survey of the World's Literature

Sylvia E. Bowman, Indiana University

GENERAL EDITOR

SOUTH AFRICA

Joseph Jones, University of Texas

EDITOR

Uys Krige

(TWAS 2)

TWAYNE'S WORLD AUTHORS SERIES (TWAS)

The purpose of TWAS is to survey the major writers —novelists, dramatists, historians, poets, philosophers, and critics—of the nations of the world. Among the national literatures covered are those of Australia, Canada, China, Eastern Europe, France, Germany, Greece, India, Italy, Japan, Latin America, New Zealand, Poland, Russia, Scandinavia, Spain, and the African nations, as well as Hebrew, Yiddish, and Latin Classical literatures. This survey is complemented by Twayne's United States Authors Series and English Authors Series.

The intent of each volume in these series is to present a critical-analytical study of the works of the writer; to include biographical and historical material that may be necessary for understanding, appreciation, and critical appraisal of the writer; and to present all material in clear, concise English—but not to vitiate the scholarly content of the work by doing so.

Uys Krige

By CHRISTINA VAN HEYNINGEN, D. Litt.

The University of Natal

With a biographical study in four chapters by

JACQUES BERTHOUD, B.A. Hons.

The University of Natal

Twayne Publishers, Inc. :: New York

Part of this book is dedicated to my brother-in-law, Jack,

JACOB ERASMUS COETZER
who, like Uys Krige, represents much that has always
been best and that still manages to survive in the
best of the Afrikaner people.

C.v.H.

Preface

We have written our little book on the predominantly Afrikaans-speaking author, Uys Krige, in the hope that it will interest Americans and South Africans alike—and, in fact, anybody who can read English. We have, therefore, very briefly summarized all the plays, told the stories of the most important poems and tales, and then tried to convey a sense of what the total impact of each is upon the reader or audience and how this impact is made. We have also explained as briefly as possible the local and political circumstances without some knowledge of which the writer and his work could not be understood.

Both of us have had the advantage of knowing Uys Krige himself very well, of hearing him tell the full story of his life in his own restless and vivid fashion, and of ourselves living through at least some of the history that has affected him. For the author of the first part of our book this has been the history of our country since 1949; for the author of the second part it has been its story from the Boer War to the present most unhappy time.

This second author owes a debt of gratitude particularly to her cousins, Cecil Higgs, late of Cape Town, now of Vermont, C.P., and to Dr. and Mrs. F. G. van der Riet, of Grahamstown, within whose cheerful and welcoming walls the whole of Part II was written, and, in being copied out, partly rewritten.

C.V.H.
J.A.B.

Contents

Chronology

1910   Uys Krige born on February 4th.

1929   Graduates from Stellenbosch University with a Bachelor of Arts degree.

1930   Reporter for the *Rand Daily Mail*, Johannesburg.

1931   Visit to England and France.

1932   Meeting with Roy Campbell.

1933   Visit to Spain.

1935   Return to South Africa.

1935   Publication of *Kentering*, first collection of poems.

1937   Marriage to Lydia Lindeque.

1938   Publication of *Magdalena Retief* (play).

1939   Broadcaster on Bureau of Information.

1940   Publication of *Rooidag* (poetry) and *Die Palmboom* (short stories); war-correspondent in the Abyssinian Campaign.

1941   War-correspondent in Egypt; captured at Sidi Rezegh.

1943   Successful escape to Allied lines; publication of *Die Einde van die Pad* (war-poems).

1944   Return to Europe.

1946   Publication of *The Way Out* (autobiography); settles in Johannesburg.

1948   Publication of *Sol y Sombra* (travel sketches).

1949   Publication of *Hart sonder Hawe* (poetry) and *Alle Paaie Gaan na Rome* (play); editorship of periodical *Vandag*.

1950   Settles in Cape Town; publication of *Vir die Luit en die Kitaar* (poetry).

1951   Publication of *Die Sluipskutter* (play), *Die Twee Lampe* (play), and *Ver in die Wêreld* (war and travel sketches).

1952   Visit to England, France, and Spain.

1953   Publication of *Die Ryk Weduwee* (play) and of *The Dream and the Desert* (short stories).

1954   Creation of a theatre company in Cape Town.

1956   Publication of *Die Goue Kring* (play).

1958   Honorary Doctorate from the University of Natal.

1959   Visit to the United States on a Carnegie scholarship.

1960   Publication of *Ballade van die Groot Begeer* (poetry), and *Roy Campbell: A Selection with a Foreword*.

1961   Publication of *Sout van die Aarde* (essays and sketches) and *Gedigte (1927-1940)* (collected poems).

1962   Publication of *Yerma* (translation) and *The Sniper* (translation of Afrikaans one-act plays).

1963   Publication of *Eluard en die Surrealisme* (translation and criticism), and *The Two Lamps* (translation of Afrikaans play).

PART I

Biographical

CHAPTER 1

Origins and Early Life

ALL TRUE writers are distinctive, but Uys Krige is especially so. He lives in a country afflicted by unique racial and political divisions; he belongs to the only European community in Africa that is not colonial in character; and he writes in a language that has had barely thirty-six years of official existence. His own talents are singularly diverse: he has achieved distinction in poetry, the drama, the essay, the short story, translation, criticism, broadcasting, and lecturing; he has a command of seven languages: he speaks and writes English perfectly, and is proficient in Dutch, French, Spanish, Italian, and Portuguese. Furthermore, like many authors who combine a lyric gift with powers of observation, he tends to write very closely out of his own experience. It would be difficult, therefore, to explain his importance as a writer without some reference to what, at first sight, may seem extraliterary considerations—questions of biography and background.

Consequently, we have divided this study into two parts. The first concerns itself with his life, and the work that grows immediately out of it; the second, with a critical survey of individual poems, plays, and short stories.

Uys Krige's[1] patriotism is as natural as it is profound. Or, to put it more accurately, it is natural because it is profound. One might adapt his recent definition of culture and say "that it is something which, when you have it, you don't talk about!" In an age that vacillates between self-aggrandizing nationalism and self-denigrating internationalism, the capacity to love one's country without disregarding its weaknesses or justifying its folly is both unfashionable and rare. Yet it is precisely this quality that has distinguished Uys Krige as a public figure in South Africa, and his discriminating loyalty reflects a central aspect of his strength and virtue as a poet. To show how deep his roots are in the history and traditions of his native land is therefore, not irrelevant.

I Family Background

His family, on his mother's as well as on his father's side, has been in South Africa for over ten generations. The original South African Krige, Wilhelm Adolph, came from Germany to the Cape of Good Hope as a Dutch East India Official in 1721, that is, only sixty-nine years after the foundation of Cape Town. In 1688 the Governor of the little colony, Simon van der Stel, had welcomed a number of Huguenot families fleeing from the persecution of Louis XIV, and had settled them in beautiful temperate valleys northeast of Cape Town. It was a de Villiers, the daughter of one of these gifted immigrants who were to make a great contribution to the growth of the country, that Wilhelm Krige married. With her, he acquired a spacious wine farm, and established himself in the vicinity of Stellenbosch.

The Kriges were never to lose their connection with this enchanting village. For almost two hundred and fifty years Kriges and Louws—Uys Krige's grandmother on his father's side was a Louw—have lived in their gabled homesteads under the Stellenbosch Mountains, surrounded by their orchards, vineyards and plantations of oak trees; and, until recently, their farms almost girdled the eastern side of the town. In the course of two centuries, the Kriges have played a distinguished part in the civil and professional life of the Western Province. It is such families that Olive Schreiner described, in 1894, as being "in the foremost rank of the nineteenth-century civilization and culture." "They are," she added, "often among our best lawyers, our best judges, our most skilful magistrates and civil servants." [2] Uys Krige's grandfather, for instance, was a Dutch Reformed Church minister of authority and great learning, and of his seven sons two became doctors, one a magistrate, one a bank manager, and one a high-school teacher.

The early population of the Cape very quickly formed itself into two rural orders: on the one hand, the comfortable landowners just described; on the other, the migrating cattle-men of the frontiers who, less cultivated but perhaps more heroic than their compatriots, lived primitive and simple lives; the latter, often exposed to danger and hardship, gradually acquired that stubbornness and love of independence by which we recognize the historical Boer. It is to this category that many of Uys Krige's maternal ancestors belong. The first Uys arrived with his wife from Friesland in 1704; his son Dirk married a Huguenot girl, and it was Dirk's son, Cornelis Janse, who in 1765 proceeded to the bare, bleak, hilly country of the Swellendam district in order to farm with sheep and cattle. As the Colony expanded, some of the Uyses moved eastwards. By the beginning of the nineteenth century they were in the Eastern Province; by 1837 Jacobus Uys and his famous son Piet were leading one of the four great Treks into the unexplored North. The temperament of the Uyses seems to have contrasted vividly with the reason and calm of the Kriges. They were a proud, vulnerable, and fiery people, often restless and melancholy, with a distinct streak of adventurousness. One could quote many examples: for instance that of the Voortrekker leader Piet Uys and his son Dirk, whose legendary deaths, after the murder of the great Voortrekker leader Piet Retief (like Piet Uys, a great-great-great-uncle of Uys Krige) are known to every South African schoolboy; or, more recently, that of his uncle, Petrus Arnoldus Uys, a big-game hunter, and the actor of daring escapades during the Anglo-Boer War.

Uys Krige has said: "My interest in my family is part of my attempt to explain myself." This "attempt" will require some tenacity, for his cousins are now as innumerable as the seed of Abraham. In fact, to be in his company for any length of time is almost comic, for one is constantly encountering new relatives. And yet his remark is not without significance: a poet whose forefathers have so remarkably contributed to his country's identity—who can, as it were, feel its past in his blood—is likely to be liberated from the self-conscious obsession to create a national literature so characteristic of the writer in a new country. He can be about the poet's proper business, the fulfilment of his most personal self, without fear or false obligations. He can write a play about modern Spain without feeling guilty. And in doing this, he will not have been disloyal: what else can a writer offer, but what he is?

II *The Father*

His father, Jacobus Daniel Krige (1879–1961), whom the son remembers as "a small, gentle man, who was never heard to disparage anyone in his life," performed for many years the duties of a magistrate in the Cape Province and the Orange Free State. Uys Krige's own tolerance and sweetness of temper are largely inherited from him, and it was his father's profession that prompted him, at the age of seventeen, to study law. It is not however J. D. Krige the magistrate that all South Africa knows, but "Japie Krige," described by some critics as the greatest rugby center-three-quarter in the history of the game.

To understand the implication of this statement, it is necessary to know that the rugby hero is to the South African public what the bullfighter is to the Spanish. The performance of the Springbok teams is almost a barometer of national self-confidence. And the reason for this prominence is not difficult to find. In 1903, less than one year after the defeat of the Boer War, South Africa won its first series of matches against a British touring team; and three years later these victories were confirmed by a dazzling visit to the British Isles. These "original Springboks," who laid the foundations of future invincibility, were associated with the recovery of national self-respect, and today are regarded as giants. The most famous of them is "Japie" Krige.

We shall see later how Uys Krige, who in his youth possessed something of his father's sporting prowess, turned it to his advantage. In the meantime, however, one should note that the sense of the open air which one constantly encounters in his work—he sometimes describes himself as "an *al fresco* writer"—he owes in some measure to the health and sanity of his early environment.

III *The Mother*

His mother, Suzanna Uys (born in 1886) is responsible for the awakening of his artistic nature. Brought up with her sisters by an English governess, she then studied music at Stellenbosch. Uys Krige describes her, in the classic Italian phrase, as *"forte e gentile"*—strong and sensitive—and again as "gracious, imaginative and vulnerable." She early conveyed her enthusiasm for the arts to her children: she took them to their first plays; introduced them to the Classics; and, to extend their education, insisted on their speaking English to her. Later her son was to repay her in kind. With his encouragement, she published at the age of sixty-two, long after her children had made their way in the world, her first volume of short stories or sketches, *Vroue* (Women). This work was followed by another collection, *Papawers en Pikkewyne* (Poppies and Penguins) and by her subsequent articles and radio talks that, under her maiden name Sannie Uys, have aroused considerable interest. Her influence on her son has been lasting and profound; an indication of it the fact that she has appeared, in various guises, as a character in many of his plays, *Magdalena Retief*, for instance, or *Alle Paaie gaan na Rome* (All Roads lead to Rome), or *Die Sluipskutter* (The Sniper).

IV *The Talented Children*

It is not surprising that such parents should have produced a consistently talented family. The eldest son, Jacobus ("Bokkie"), born a year after their marriage in 1908, won a Rhodes Scholarship and studied English at Oxford. Now a high-ranking aviator, he has made two fine translations into Afrikaans of Antoine de St. Exupéry: *Vol de Nuit* and *Terre des Hommes*. Uys, the second son, was born on February 4, 1910, and was followed a year later by Arnold, a cultured and widely traveled man. Three years later saw the arrival of François, who at a very early age began to show ability with the pencil and brush. He is now recognized as one of the best local artists (Sir John Rothenstein has called him "the finest draftsman in South Africa"). He has exhibited with success at the Venice *Biennale*, and he has illustrated many books, notably the travel sketches of his brother, and of Johan van der Post. These four brothers were followed by two sisters: Maria Magdalena (Mizzi) in 1917; Suzanne, in 1926. The former, before her early death, showed considerable ability as an actress; the latter is married to the brilliant South African architect, Revel Fox.

If one considers what it must have meant to share one's early years with such gay and talented companions—those who recall their carefree days on the splendid Cape beaches always seem to evoke the breath of an ideal and forgotten world—one is scarcely surprised to find in Uys Krige's work the candor and simplicity of feeling that often comes from secure origins. Despite his understanding of the darker side of life, he has never lost his buoyancy and joy: whatever its theme or subject, his work is that of a happy man.

V *The Setting*

Accompanying his capacity for enjoyment is a certain fanciful-
ness and romanticism which the landscapes of his boyhood must
have helped to foster. His maternal grandfather's farm, "Bontebokskloof" (The Kloof of the Dappled Deer) on which he was
born—"a most beautiful farm at the foot of the towering Lange-
berg"—and the nearby "melancholy coast" of Cape Infanta provided the setting for his play, *Die Twee Lampe* (The Two
Lamps), and also inspired several short stories, notably the famous "The Coffin" and "The Two Children." At an early age, he
moved to the Karroo, the vast semi-desert in the middle of the
Cape Province where the celebrated "open spaces" of South Africa can be most vividly experienced. When he says of the friend-
liness and informality of certain South Africans that "they participate in the generosity of their horizons," he is obviously thinking
of the serene atmosphere and the enormous distances of that
landscape. After two years on a farm near Cape Agulhas, the
southernmost point of the continent of Africa—an incident of that
period provoked the short story "Die Stad" (The City)—the
Kriges went to live near Cape Town where, for the first time, Uys
went to an English-medium school. The atmosphere of boyhood
games at that time is wonderfully captured in some of the
sketches in *Sout van die Aarde* (Salt of the Earth).

He spent his early childhood, then, only in the country, and it is
perhaps because of this that he has shown in his work as a whole a
marked preference for a rural setting. All his plays, for example,
unfold against a country background, and very few of his poems
and short stories refer to the city and its problems.

VI *Reading, Education, Writing*

At the age of fourteen, after his father had been transferred to
Stellenbosch, the ancestral town of the Kriges, he began to read
poetry for himself. He spent ten years there, first at the celebrated
parallel-medium[3] Paul Roos Gymnasium, then at the University
of Stellenbosch. The graciousness, serenity and *savoir vivre* of
Stellenbosch life at the time made a profound impression on him;
and his recollections of Stellenbosch and of districts like it have
inspired two of his finest works, the autobiographical nouvelle

"The Dream," and, less directly, the enchanting comedy *Die Ryk Weduwee* (The Rich Widow).

He discovered poetry under the tutelage of his first English high-school teacher, the Reverend P. J. Loseby, and he started reading the English Romantics. At the age of fifteen he was contributing English prose and Afrikaans poetry to such reviews as *The Cape* and *De Goede Hoop.* Very early he began to reveal his undoubted descriptive powers, and started to knit what was to become a life-long association with literary journals and periodicals.

In 1927, he registered for the Bachelor of Arts course in law at the University of Stellenbosch. Although he graduated normally three years later, the standard of his academic work dropped sharply after he had left school. This, however, is not surprising. At the age of seventeen his interest in literature had superseded all other interests: instead of studying law, he devoured every slim volume of modern Dutch and English poetry he could find. Then, in his first year at the university, he fell under the influence of J. M. L. Franken, the professor of French language and literature; and the treasures of French poetry began to open before him. Later, he was to show his gratitude by dedicating his first book of translations to him. In the meantime, Uys Krige rapidly explored Vigny, Prudhomme, and the Parnassians. Soon he was absorbing the great poets Villon, Baudelaire, Rimbaud, Verlaine, Mallarmé, and—what is astonishing at that date—Apollinaire. He also discovered Daudet and de Maupassant, some of whose short stories he began to translate for *Die Huisgenoot,* a weekly magazine. At the same period, Professor F. E. J. Malherbe was delivering his popular lectures on the Impressionists and Post Impressionists, and this, combined with the fact that his brother François had now entered the Fine Art school at Cape Town, served to awaken in Uys a fierce desire to experience French culture directly. He continued, however, to work as a freelance journalist, publishing articles in the Cape Town daily papers. By the time he was graduating, he had made up his mind: he would become a writer, not an advocate.

VII   *Development of Afrikaans*

It is necessary, as Uys Krige's literary career is discussed, to indicate the level of development attained by the language he was to use. Originating with the Dutch dialects of the seventeenth century, and unrestrained by the conserving influences of schools and books, or by frequent contact with the mother country, the vernacular now known as Afrikaans evolved very rapidly. At the turn of the nineteenth century, it had become the spoken language of the Boer. In 1876, an association dedicated to the promotion of Afrikaans created the first literary monthly, *Die Afrikaanse Patriot*. The Anglo-Boer War accelerated the process, and the first dictionary appeared in 1902. From then on, Afrikaans struggled against Dutch for official recognition: in 1918, it was elevated to national status; and finally, in 1925, it replaced its rival in the Houses of Parliament.

This language, analytic in form, and enriched by contact with such indigenous dialects as Hottentot and by the imported idiom of the Portuguese-Malay slaves, was ready for the dignity that only literature can confer. In the words of Roy Campbell: "The Afrikaans language . . . is full of adventure for the bold and daring . . . and unique among contemporary tongues for youth and freshness." [4] This adventure Uys Krige was to feel at once with special intensity; as the second part of this study shows, his vocabulary and syntax are filled with the excitement of helping to create a language. (See Appendix.)

What traditions did Afrikaans literature have to offer to the young poet of the late 1920's? Looking about him, he would have found a sprinkling of folk-ballads from the Cape Colored community, a quantity of declarations in patriotic verse, a few earnest bucolic pieces. He could read, indeed, the poetry of Eugène Marais, Jan Celliers, Totius, C. Louis Leipoldt and A. G. Visser, men of feeling, ability, and wide culture. But beyond this, there was little to absorb the attention of someone seriously interested in literature.

So it was, in part at least, the poverty of his own literary traditions that turned Uys Krige to the Old World. In this respect, of course, he resembled several of his own contemporaries; but there are two important differences. His fellow-poets found their inspiration in England and, more particularly, in Holland and Flanders; Uys Krige at once discovered his affinities with the culture of the Romance language countries. Again, as with others, the study of foreign literatures often arose out of a deliberate policy to construct a national literature; in his case, it came with the force of a spontaneous revelation. His discovery of Europe was part of no program: it was, on the contrary, a discovery of himself.

VIII *Reporter*

By the time he had taken his degree, Uys Krige found himself in a very restless and unsettled frame of mind. After a brief visit to the Eastern Province, to which his father had been transferred two years previously, he decided not to take the further degree necessary for the completion of his legal studies; and, instead of returning with his friends to Stellenbosch, he made his way to Johannesburg, from where he had vague plans of finding a passage to Europe.

He had barely arrived at the Witwatersrand, however, when he was offered a position as a reporter on the *Rand Daily Mail,* the well known daily paper established by Edgar Wallace. So began a period of eighteen months during which for the first time he experienced life in an aggressive mining metropolis. To share flats with a number of tough, able journalists—many of whom were later to achieve fame as international correspondents—and to participate in the hectic competitive excitement of a city in full boom did much to strengthen the self-reliance which has enabled him, since then, to survive on nothing but the proceeds of his pen. But he soon learned that this existence was dangerous, if not destructive, to his nascent poetic talent. In July of 1931, therefore, he assembled his savings, took leave of his family; and, in the company of John Barkham—a fellow reporter who is now editor of the New York *Saturday Review Syndicate*—he set sail for his first great adventure.

CHAPTER 2

First Visit to Europe

NOTHING in Uys Krige's life—unless one includes his experience of World War II—can rival in importance the four and a half years he was to spend in France and in Spain. It was there he was to discover the full range and power of literature, to learn the nature of his tastes and values, and to recognize the direction of his political beliefs. It was there too that he was to serve his early apprenticeship as a poet and a stylist.

In addition to this, he has recorded many of his impressions in a number of sketches and essays, some early, some more recent, but all written in the supple, racy, lucid prose that so vividly reflects the spontaneity and charm of his personality: "Rugby in Frankryk" (Rugby in France), "Eerste Ontmoeting met Roy Campbell" (First Meeting with Roy Campbell), "Die Venesie van Provence" (The Venice of Provence), "Die Oponthoud" (The Breakdown), "Valenciaanse Uitstappie" (Valencia Outing)—to quote but those that have appeared in book form—and the studies written in Spain, *Sol y Sombra* (Sun and Shadow—the name given to the intermediate seats in the bullring). This period, therefore, warrants rather detailed treatment; and this chapter reflects, if only indirectly, the substance of his autobiographical pieces.

I *Impressions of England: Effect of France*

His first impressions of England were inauspicious. The weather was appalling; the forty pounds he had in his pocket were rapidly melting away; and his elder brother, then at Oxford, was holidaying in Austria. Uys' anxiety was increased by the thought of the coming winter: if *this* was an English July, what would November bring? He would take the first opportunity to flee. He has described how an English sporting journalist told him, one wet afternoon in a little Fleet Street cafe, that he would find himself more at home in the South of France. There he would have sunlight even in winter; and, since the local population was "crazy about rugby" (France had just defeated England for the first time), he might even earn a little pocket money if he managed to get into a team. He had only to remember that Provence was the land of Cézanne and van Gogh, de Maupassant and Daudet, to make the suggestion irresistible. He consulted a map: near the Italian frontier, he found Nice; then, further west, the French military harbor of Toulon; and, a few miles beyond, Marseille. These last two towns were famous rugby centers; between them was the little fishing village of Sanary-sur-Mer. He would leave England at once.

Three weeks later—he had been delayed in Paris, where he had met his brother—he was receiving his first glimpses of a beautiful Provence afternoon: the pure sky of the south, the mountains, the Mediterranean, and later, as he walked from the station, the grey olive groves, the scattered pine trees, and the fragrance of the grape harvest.

This landscape has been immortalized by the Impressionists, and since then has attracted painters from all parts of the world. Sanary, for instance, has harbored such artists as André Dérain, De Segonzac, and Moïse Kisling. But it is not always realized that the "côte d'azur" has been the scene of so much foreign literary activity. D. H. Lawrence, for instance, spent the last years of his life at Bandol, two miles from the village of Uys Krige's choice; Scott Fitzgerald passed his happiest days at Antibes, only a few miles further. Uys Krige could meet people such as Aldous Huxley, and live, as he puts it, "from the street up," listening to idiomatic French, picking up casual acquaintances, (he has quite a gift that way), and observing about him all the ebullient goings-on of the *Provençaux*. Under the enormous stimulus of this new environment, his talent immediately began to flower. Through the next two years, he was to compose the bulk of the poetry that appeared in his first two collections, *Kentering* (Turningpoint) and *Rooidag* (Daybreak). But in the meantime, he could not survive on rhyme alone.

A few days after his arrival at Sanary, he went into Toulon, found his way to the local rugby club, and was accepted for a couple of practices. The following Sunday he was playing as center-three-quarter for the first team of the most powerful club in

France: Toulon had been the 1930–31 national champions, and contained several international players. The next morning, he opened the papers to find himself famous. And so it came about that he acquired a reputation as a rugby player before he had published a single important line of verse.

A period of great excitement and glamor now opened. Possessed of perfect health and an enormous zest, ready for any adventure, and filled with the youthful confidence that lets the future look after itself, he traveled the length and breadth of Provence, and explored its every corner. During the Christmas season of 1931, he toured France itself while accompanying his team to such cities as Dijon, Lyons, and Paris. His lionization in the grandiloquent French sporting press is most amusingly described in the first sketch of *Sout van die Aarde* (Salt of the Earth). The whole essay, in fact, breathes the atmosphere of gay Bohemianism and of casual comradeship that was the mark of these wonderful days.

Even more Bohemian was the summer of 1932, for, with the end of the rugby season, came the end of food and pocket money. He found himself at Nice, then more than now the playground of the international set, and filled with the corrupt glitter of pleasure-seekers and with the artistic fringe. In rapid succession, he performed the duties of a "plongeur," or hotel dishwasher; of a linoleum salesman for a Corsican; and of an extra in Papst's historic film *Don Quixote*. He finally became a swimming teacher in the employment of a devious Armenian who set him up on the beach under a larger poster showing a flexed bicep and the following legend:—Uys Krije—"Champion de France"—"Professeur de Natation et de Culture Physique." He spent June and July all day on the sand, was burnt black by the sun, but his shock of golden hair turned white in the glare; he was trying to induce aristocratic young ladies to learn the elements of the backstroke. This refreshing occupation ended suddenly when, ironically enough—for he was full of unspoilt innocence, a quality he has retained to a surprising degree—he was sacked on a trumped-up charge of immorality. Two indignant friends immediately espoused his cause; and, to his embarrassment, they began to engage in a real vendetta against the Armenian. To avoid further imbroglios, Uys decided to take the train to Marseille.

In this teeming, unclean, raucous city, he resumed with the return of the winter season his sporting profession, coaching and playing for the local club. He experienced moments of loneliness, but they seem to have had a positive effect, for, at the end of that year, he was writing poetry almost daily. At the same time, he started sending potted articles on Provençal life to the South African press. All his work was done in bars and restaurants, where he would sit with pen and paper for hours, surrounded by the warmth and companionship of patrons and regulars. But, before Christmas of 1932, two incidents—one of them of the greatest importance—put an end to this mode of existence.

II   *Italy; Roy Campbell*

One winter evening, as he was crossing a square, a figure caught his attention. He overtook it, stopped it—it was J. M. L. Franken, his French professor from Stellenbosch! In the pleasure of the reunion, Professor Franken invited him to accompany him on a visit to Italy. For the next three weeks he explored the architecture and art treasures of Rome, Naples, Genoa, Pisa, and Florence. This was his first taste of a country which was later to make a very different impression on him.

The second incident had taken place before his meeting with Franken. He had known for some time that a fellow South African, Roy Campbell, was living at Martigues, a picturesque fishing village situated about thirty miles to the west of Marseille. Having read *The Wayzgoose* and *Adamastor,* he was eager to meet their creator. He has written a fine description of his visit to Campbell: his first impressions of the Cézanne country—the hills of l'Estaque, the Mont St. Victoire and the lake of Berre, on the edge of which Campbell had his olive farm; of the impact of Campbell's broad, exuberant personality; of their mutual enthusiasm for Provence and French poetry; of their ride into Martigues; and of their first conversation under the plane trees. Soon he was visiting the Campbells regularly; this led to a firm friendship and in March of the following year he went to live with them as a tutor to their children.

This relationship had a profound and lasting effect on Uys Krige. When asked recently what he had found so impressive about Campbell, he replied: "I saw generosity in action." The unrestrained freedom with which Campbell spoke about his craft, his work, and his knowledge, overwhelmed him. He added, "I understood that the tradition of poetic craft is like a golden chain handed down to the young." With this generosity he also encountered, for the first time, the unworldliness and discipline of the artist. He watched a man, one who had sacrificed ease and comfort for the integrity of his work, toil endlessly over his manuscripts. He learned the lesson of complete dedication.

Perhaps the fact that Campbell recognized in Uys Krige the pattern of his own development—they had independently followed the same path of discovery through the poetry of France—explains, in part at least, the suddenness of the friendship. Under Campbell's inspiration, Uys Krige began to enlarge his reading. He discovered the big novel—*Moby Dick, War and Peace, Don Quixote*—and the literature of the great French classical period—Corneille, Racine, Molière. With Campbell's encouragement, he started to write an epic poem, of which only fragments have been published since the completed manuscript was stolen from him in a Spanish train a year later. So deeply was he stirred by the year spent with Campbell, that his loyalty and gratitude have never wavered. Twenty-eight years later, in his preface to a selection of Campbell's poetry, his enthusiasm is as evident as ever: "Of (his) poetry I should like to say, finally, that whatever its faults, . . . when all the cliques, claques and coteries of our time have settled into their rightful little grooves, Roy Campbell will stand out as one of the finest lyrical voices of his generation. . . ." [1]

As this sojourn in Provence is about to come to an end, it might not be inopportune to review very briefly the nature and scope of his debt to it. In many ways, it was an essentially assimilative period. His ear was eagerly tuned to the racy idiom of Provençal French to see how it could enrich the expressiveness of his native Afrikaans. He devoured newspapers and literary reviews such as the *Nouvelle Revue Française* and *Cahiers du Sud* to discover the secret of good prose. French prose, in fact, prepared him for the work he was to do in Spain: "The clarity," he says, "jumped out of the page." Conversation with brilliant people, and contact with a level of culture very different from that he had been accustomed to, transformed his mind and taste. Today, despite the ease with which he carries it, his erudition has an astonishing range; and it is accompanied by considerable (though not always infallible) powers of self-criticism.

[26]

The influence of the French poets pervades the lyrics he was writing at that time. Apart from the fine translations he was working on, one can easily detect in his original work the effect of Villon, Baudelaire, Rimbaud, and Apollinaire. Baudelaire's is paramount; indeed, Krige confesses to having been almost obsessed by him. This influence is not direct—that is, he does not copy the imagery and diction—but it can be felt in the musicality of his verse and in the texture of his emotion. An attentive reading of "Dagbreek" (Daybreak) with "Le crépuscule du matin," (The Twilight of Morning) or of "Die Swerwers" (The Vagabonds) with "Le Voyage," for instance, will make this clear. Krige says that Baudelaire revealed to him the movement of a great lyric, the subtle "rhythm within the rhythm" that, set in motion by the first phrase of the poem, gathers power and momentum until, with the final line, it "comes home smoothly, like the keel of a boat slipping onto the sand." Clear too, on some of the early ballads, is the mark of Villon. Again, form and situation in the poem "Afspraak" (Appointment) are derived from Rimbaud's "Les Reparties de Nina"; the celebrated "Tram-Ode" (Tram Ode) is fundamentally anteceded by Apollinaire's "Zone." But a reading of Uys Krige's early poems will convince the discriminating critic that he did not steal from the great French poets: he learned from them.

III *Spain*

During the latter part of 1933, his thoughts had increasingly turned towards Spain. He had started learning Spanish in the company of Campbell's wife, and was already reading Latin-American verse—for, as he says himself, a poet always learns a language where it is most terse, memorable, and expressive. Furthermore, Campbell had been growing poorer and poorer; and, when he heard that life across the Pyrenees was very much cheaper than in France, where the cost of living was rising, he needed little persuasion to move. At the end of November, therefore, they decided to go to Barcelona.

Uys Krige arrived in Spain at perhaps the most critical moment of this dramatic nation's history. Thirty months later, the country was to explode into civil war. In December, 1933, it was a seething confusion of political crosscurrents. The Second Republic, which on a surge of idealistic popular suffrage had succeeded the mili-

tary dictatorship of Primo de Rivera, was in the process of disintegrating. The left-wing government, which had antagonized every
group—first, by its proposed reforms; then, by its failure to carry
them out—was about to be replaced by a center-right coalition.
Barcelona itself was a melting-pot of conflicting party loyalties.
Both the extreme left—the Anarchists, Communists, and the Socialists, whose power rested on the discontent of the workers and
the peasantry—and the extreme right consisting of the Church
and the Capitalists, the landowners, and the Fascist-oriented
army-juntas were bitterly opposed, not only to each other, but
also to the central government. This confusion was twice con-
founded by the presence of yet another enemy to Madrid, the
Catalan separatists, who, inspired by six centuries of proud
achievement, both commercial and artistic (Renaissance Barcelona had rivalled Venice and Genoa, and Catalan culture could
now boast of such luminaries as the musician Casals, the architect
Gaudí, and the poets Verdaguer and Ribas) were clamoring for
greater autonomy. This situation makes itself felt behind every
page of the collection of sketches, *Sol y Sombra,* that arose out of
that period. Shootings in the street, daily bomb explosions, and
massive political demonstrations form the background of the first
part of this book.

Uys Krige started writing it under the most extraordinary circumstances. Having parted from the Campbells, who were now
too poor to admit another member to their family, he went to live
in the notorious Barrio Chino, the underworld district of the city
where very cheap meals could be acquired. Part of *Sol y Sombra*
describes this haunt of beggars and confidence-tricksters, pimps
and prostitutes, and political refugees from every quarter of Europe who, engaged even here in espionage and counter-espionage,
added a clandestine flavor to the already lurid atmosphere. His
troubles, increased by the most ferocious winter in years, culmi-
nated with the theft of his wallet containing his last resources. It
was then that it occurred to him to exploit his new found skill in
writing prose by sending a series of articles, this time based directly on his own experience, to the South African press.

But the first payment for these would not arrive for three
months, and he was suffering moments of extreme hunger, when,
as he stood on a street corner, his ears would suddenly start singing. So an Italian friend, the writer Alberto Colini, whom he had

met and helped soon after his arrival in Barcelona, and who, with his experience as an exile from Fascist Italy, had evolved a technique of living on nothing, offered to assist him. For a while, therefore, Krige was supported by a man who was, in his turn, supported by a syndicate of professional beggars. Augmenting this income with occasional gifts of food from Spanish grocers and Dutch sailors, Krige weathered the winter and, with the arrival of the first check, decided to move south. The spring of 1934 found him in Valencia. Here, under the warm skies, and amidst the flower gardens, orange groves, and exotic architecture of this ancient seat of learning—some of the most enchanting chapters of *Sol y Sombra* evoke the beauty of its Moorish buildings and subtropical vegetation—the quality of his sketches began to improve. At that time, if one excepts Eugene Marais's *Siel van die Mier* (Soul of the Ant) and a few other works, Afrikaans prose of any quality was practically non-existent. Krige now felt, with great excitement, that "the language was beginning to tremble in his hand," and in that mood he started to prepare his first collection of poems for the press.

It was in Valencia, too, that Spanish literature made its full impact. He attended classes for a while at its famed university, but when, after an outburst of shooting, the university was closed down, he rented a cottage in the fishing quarter of Malvarossa, a district favored by writers which Hemingway has described in *Death in the Afternoon*. If Spain was disintegrating politically, it was, on the other hand, experiencing an extraordinary outburst of artistic creation. Provoked by the essays and other writings of the so-called "generation of 1898"—a group of philosophers, critics, and writers such as Unamuno, Azorín, Ortega, and Baroja, whose criticism of the Spanish character had transformed the intellectual life of the country—there had arisen a host of talented playwrights and poets, notably Benavente and García Lorca in the fields of realistic and poetic drama, respectively, and the lyric poets Jiménez, Machado, Alberti, and of course Lorca himself—to name but a few. It is difficult to overestimate the importance that these writers came to assume for Krige; an attempt will be made, later, to assess it briefly. At this point, however, one may remark that Spain did to his heart and feelings what France had done to his mind and taste. He was joined in late midsummer by his young brother, François, who had been studying painting in

Madrid; and together they toured the great cities of Castile. Spain, with all its passionate austerity and colossal artistic achievement, opened before him in a never-forgotten revelation.

In December, 1934, he moved again, this time to Almería, a little town on the southern coast, backed by the foothills of the Sierra Nevada. Formerly an Arab arsenal of strategic importance, it had now something of the abandoned leisureliness of a city forgotten by the twentieth century. Having come into a legacy of about £100, Krige was able to lead, for once, a life of almost bourgeois "amplitude." He rented a house overlooking the Mediterranean, invited his brother to share it with him, and quietly began to absorb the traditions of Andalusia by studying its rich past and even richer present. While François was exploring the local landscape with pen and palette, Uys steeped himself in the work of García Lorca, particularly in his play *Mariana Pineda* and his famous collection of ballads *Romancero Gitano,* both of which were already becoming Republican declarations of faith. So passed five months of pleasure and companionship.

The arrival of his mother on a brief visit to Europe, however, caused a new spate of vagabondage. Having accompanied her on a short tour of central Spain and Provence, he proceeded to Antwerp alone and spent most of the summer in Belgium. Returned to Madrid in August, he started to plan a book on Goya and attended performances of the plays of the classic dramatists, Lope de Vega and Calderon. However, a longing for South Africa began to assert itself. He had been rootless for too long and had reached saturation point. Further dislocated by the failure of an emotional relationship formed in Valencia the year before, he spent the last three weeks with the Campbells at Toledo. In December, 1935, four and a half years after his arrival in Europe and six months before the outbreak of the Civil War, he returned to South Africa.

If France had given him *joie de vivre,* Spain had provided an experience brooding and somber. In fact, the two years spent in that country had seared themselves into his being. The Iberian landscape, with its coasts and plateaux so reminiscent of his native land; the splendors of the art and literature; the pride and passion of the people; and Spain's violent, dramatic history, which was so soon to repeat itself into a new and appalling episode—all these had fallen upon him with the force of an explosion. It was in

Barcelona that he discovered himself as a prose writer, and in Madrid that he first sensed the possibilities of the theater. And it was in Spain too, in the Republican strongholds of the western coasts, while sharing life with poets and intellectuals and while mixing with workers, peasants, fishermen, and artisans, that the foundations of his sympathy for the ordinary man were laid—and his steadfast opposition to tyranny in all its forms.

CHAPTER 3

World War II

FOR Uys Krige, the period that preceded the great conflict of 1939 was in many respects one of consolidation; but in other ways it seems to have been a time of preparation for the role he was to play in World War II. It is, therefore, legitimate to include it in a chapter principally devoted to his war experience.

On his return to South Africa, he found the country in a state of prosperity and development. The two traditional political groups, the South African Party under General Smuts and the Nationalist Party under General Hertzog, had coalesced to form a new combination, the United Party. The extreme wing of the Nationalist Party, led by Dr. Malan, had refused to cooperate and continued to be the repository of ancient grudges and resentments only too easily fanned by German propaganda; but nothing as yet seriously threatened the harmony of the nation.

Occasional publication, particularly of Krige's poetry and the travel sketches from Spain, had already earned him a measure of prestige. Of the latter, for instance, Jacques Malan had said: "A prose full of winged neologisms and supple rhythms . . . which dulled the contents of the columns accompanying it into drab death." His first collection of verse, *Kentering* (Turningpoint), which had appeared in Pretoria during 1935, had been warmly received. He had therefore no great difficulty in acquiring congenial employment. After spending a few recuperative months with his parents at Ladybrand, a small Free State town near the Caledon river ("rich maize-lands of great skies in which clouds changed as if a sculptor was fashioning them"), where he wrote the celebrated patriotic poem "Verre Blik" (Distant View) and the stirring "Die Rit van Jan Lafras Malherbe" (Jan Lafras Malherbe's ride), he was appointed literary editor of *Die Vaderland*, a Johannesburg newspaper supporting Hertzog and enjoying, in those days, a considerable reputation.

I *Marriage*

It was in Johannesburg that he met his future wife, Lydia Lindeque, one of the three or four important names of the Afrikaans
stage. She has written an amusing and lively memoir, *Trek op die
Skerm* (Pull up the Curtain). Leaving school at an early age, she
joined the company created by Paul de Groot, a Hollander generally regarded as the pioneer of the Afrikaans theater; went on her
first tour at the age of seventeen; and by 1936 was playing regularly in Johannesburg with such actors as Andre Huguenet. When
Uys Krige met her, he was twenty-six; she was two years younger
—a handsome woman whom he describes as "arrestingly beautiful." He immediately fell under the spell of her powerful, direct
personality. To her he owes the awakening of his desire to write
plays. He had always had a flair for the dramatic and a strong, if
latent, sense of audience—one feels, for instance, even in his
lyrics, that his language is a spoken language—but she was responsible for focussing his attention on the theater.

They were married early in the following year and settled in
Cape Town, a city which he has since, despite long intervals of
absence, considered his home. There he met a few talented South
African artists, such as Wolf Kibel and Lippy Lipschitz; and he
began to associate with a number of Afrikaans poets, later to be
somewhat artificially classified as the "poets of the thirties," a
group supposedly sensitive to European influences and to the new
movement in poetry.[6] Uys Krige, however, has never been properly assimilated into this category: he is far too spontaneous, too
individual, and too indifferent to literary politics.

Marriage very soon began to give a direction to his literary activity. He was then the literary editor of the Cape Town newspaper, *Die Suiderstem;* but, with his wife's encouragement, he
gradually relinquished formal work in order to devote his energies
to writing for the stage. Starting with two short radio dialogues,
Die Gees van die Water (The Spirit of the Water) and *Die
Skaapwagters van Bethlehem* (The Shepherds of Bethlehem)—
the latter coinciding with the birth of his daughter Eulalia on
Christmas Day, 1937—he had composed by the following year his
first full-length play, *Magdalena Retief,* an episodic drama on the
Voortrekkers. This play was quickly followed by two one-act
plays, *Die Wit Muur* (The White Wall), based on an incident of

the Boer War, and *Die Arrestasie* (The Arrest), a miniature comedy of manners set in the early days of Stellenbosch. At that time, he was very much, to use his own phrase, "the blue-eyed boy"; his plays had an effective, if simple, patriotic appeal; his *Magdalena Retief* was being performed in the Transvaal, and won a first prize; and his poems and short stories were appearing everywhere. But this popularity was not to last.

II *Spanish Civil War*

In July, 1936, news reached South Africa that civil war had broken out in Spain. Although he had already learned to suspect the nature of Fascism, it was only when the Spanish garrisons began to revolt all over the country that Krige woke up to its full implications. The crowded and often confused impressions stored in his mind during his European visit suddenly dovetailed, and he began to understand something of the nature of the forces that would soon mobilize the manhood of the entire civilized world. He became obsessed by the Spanish situation. He considered enlisting in the International Brigade, but the Spanish ambassador discouraged him by telling him that the Republican cause needed advocates abroad and particularly in South Africa, where the Afrikaans Nationalist Press was presenting Franco as a nationalist hero. In 1937, accordingly, Krige became a member of a committee formed for the relief of Spanish children; and he forced himself to take the unprecedented step of publicly interpreting the course of the Civil War. This first commitment was accompanied by intense, private literary activity. Early that year, he completed his translation of Lorca's *Mariana Pineda;* then followed his superb version of the same author's famous lament for the death of the bullfighter, the "Llanto por Ignacio Sánchez Mejías," and Krige's own well known "Lied van die Fascistiese Bomwerpers" (Song of the Fascist Bombers), infinitely more striking, in its complexity and exaltation than, for instance, Campbell's unilinear lyrics against the Republicans at the siege of Toledo. By the beginning of 1940, Krige had written a further play, *Fuente Sagrada,* on a theme arising out of his desire to participate in the Civil War. These efforts, however, did him little local harm; the Spanish conflict was too remote and too unreal to kindle violent feelings at home.

[34]

III   *War on Germany*

When Britain declared war on Germany, on September 3, 1939, however, the situation was immediately transformed. The crisis into which the South African cabinet was plunged was resolved three days later with Smuts's victory over Hertzog's policy of neutrality and over Malan's manifest antagonism; and South Africa declared war in its turn. But the temper of the country was such that Smuts did not dare enforce conscription.

Uys Krige was then earning his living as a freelance journalist on the Witwatersrand. At the end of 1939, he was appointed by Smuts as an Afrikaans broadcaster with Arthur N. Wilson, his English equivalent, to the newly created Bureau of Information—ironically enough the ancestor of the present mammoth Ministry of Information. The earlier antipropaganda organ was designed to combat "Zeesen," the Nazi station whose powerful transmitters had for some time been beamed to local receiving sets. Krige's daily attacks over the air on Nazi Germany immediately flung him into prominence, and the Nationalist press was not slow to react. A prominent weekly that Krige had helped found in 1936 discontinued his unfinished series of articles on Basutoland; the headlines of others poured abuse on him—some of his less unsavory titles being "Kakieridder" (knight in khaki), "Hans-kakie" (renegade), "Loyal Dutch," "Rooiluis" (red louse), etc. Virulently attacked in the editorials of *Die Transvaler,* Dr. Verwoerd's newly created right-wing newspaper, Krige defended himself on the grounds that the menace of Hitler overshadowed party loyalties. This statement brought a torrent of imprecation to *Die Transvaler's* correspondence columns, and there ensued a systematic program of discrimination and disapproval. However, Krige continued undeterred, even when cut in the streets by former friends; and he broadcast both on the fall of Holland and on the collapse of France.

Two facts may perhaps serve to epitomize the South African situation at the beginning of the war. First, of the entire roll of Afrikaans authors of significance, only three declared themselves unambiguously against Hitler: Uys Krige, Jan van Melle, and the veteran poet, C. Louis Leipoldt. Second, all four of the Krige brothers enlisted and achieved distinction in North Africa: Bokkie, who became an airforce colonel; Uys, a war-correspondent, Arnold, an intelligence officer; and François, a war artist.

It was only with Mussolini's entry into the war in June, 1940, and the spread of the conflict to African soil, that South Africa began to participate actively. A division of infantry—enlarged with technical troops, air squadrons, and armored companies— was posted to the East African campaign. From its base, Nairobi, its objective was to capture the Axis capital Addis Ababa by means of a double advance, one from the south, the other from the north-east.

Eager to participate personally in the great experience of his compatriots and to testify to it by describing what they felt, did, and thought under the stress of war, Uys Krige asked Smuts to allow him, since he had not received military training, to go to the front as a correspondent. He arrived in Nairobi in November and at once set off in pursuit of the offensive through northern Kenya and southern Abyssinia. The revelation of Africa in all its primeval beauty, the impact of the immense deserts of the Northern Frontier District of Kenya, and the extraordinary sense of purity and comradeship of those early days are reflected in the poetry documenting them. Transferring his attention to the northeastern invasion, Krige caught up with Dan Pienaar's forces at Harrar (the town made famous by Rimbaud's residence there) and was among the first six men to enter Addis Ababa. With the end of the campaign in May, 1941, he fell violently ill and was returned to South Africa with the wounded. The poems of that period, two of which were composed in the Addis Ababa hospital, have been gathered in *Die Einde van die Pad* (The End of the Road).

On his recovery, he returned to Pretoria; but his constitutional restlessness quickly reasserted itself. Two South African divisions were now engaged in the North African campaign, where the Allies were preparing their first counteroffensive against the positions gained by Rommel's attack earlier that year. Once again, Krige obtained permission to join the army; and he arrived in September in Cairo where, for a while, he edited a weekly magazine for the troops. A group of impressionistic sketches written during that period has been preserved in *Ver in die Wêreld* (Far in the World): once again, his observant eye, his ear for dialogue, and his vivid sense of language evoke, with far greater suggestive power than a sustained narrative, the atmosphere of that time—a bombardment of Cairo, studies of individual soldiers, the sights and sounds of the desert, a sketch of a general, the oppressive delay of the big offensive.

Incapable, as usual, of remaining at base and eager to report, the attack which had at last been launched, he left Cairo on the first of November and drove into the desert. General Auchinleck's first objective was the relief of Tobruk. On November 19, Sidi Rezegh, a strategic spot southeast of the besieged stronghold, was captured by the Allies; and a savage conflict ensued. Uys Krige witnessed this battle for three days, often from very exposed positions. He has called it "assuredly the most far-reaching (ingrypende) and fundamental event of my life." [2] On Sunday, November 23, Nazi panzer units overwhelmed the defenses and encircled an entire South African brigade. Krige found himself among the captured.

His account of this incident in the essay "Totensonntag" (the day on which it took place was the traditional Lutheran "day of the dead") in *Sout van die Aarde* is one of his most brilliant prose pieces: tense and powerful, it sets down without the slightest falsification the essence of one of those heightened situations in which every detail becomes memorable. In the same way as it has been impossible, in a survey such as this one, to give an adequate idea of the richness and variety of his experiences in East and North Africa, so his essay can only earn a passing comment. But it might well be recommended to the local critics who, from the comfort of their civilian armchairs, have made the extraordinary claim that Krige writes superficially about the war.

IV Prisoner of War

A new period, one to end with his escape from a prisoner-of-war camp two years later, now began. The captured, formed into a huge column of fifteen hundred men, marched for three days in conditions of great deprivation and danger to the port of embarkation. This journey raised Uys Krige to his high moment of responsibility. The column was without officers and leadership; so he and a friend, by virtue of their knowledge of Italian and German, respectively, found themselves confronted with the task of conducting the men and maintaining their morale. The prisoners, constantly harried—first by the Tobruk artillery, then by their own airplanes and navy, and finally by British submarines—were transported by sea from Benghazi to Taranto, then transferred to a temporary camp at Brindisi. There, with very little food and with practically no blankets, they spent the darkest part of an iron winter. Uys Krige comforted himself with writing poetry; and, prompted by the fact that he was now hearing only English, he tried to write English verse. The first two poems of *Hart Sonder Hawe* (Heart without Haven) reveal something of what he had to endure.

Early in 1942, he was finally removed to a large "British" camp near Sulmona, a little town in the Abruzzi Mountains about seventy miles east of Rome. There, in what became known as the "Fonte d'Amore Camp" because of its proximity to the fountain so melodiously sung of by Ovid, Krige continued to suffer the rigors of the weather: continuous snow fell for six weeks, seven inch icicles hung from the gutters, and wolves could be heard on the cliffs overhead. To add to his discomfort, a further mishap occurred: in retaliation against similar Allied abuses, the Italians disregarded the officer status of the captured correspondents and quartered them among the men. Except for Uys Krige, they were restored to privilege in the spring after British and American attitudes had changed; but Krige had lost his identification card at Sidi Rezegh and was therefore condemned to spend an additional year in cramped crowded conditions. This situation was to prove, however, a reprieve in disguise: being the only correspondent not to be taken to northern Italy, he was the only one who managed to escape successfully.

When one converses with him, one is constantly aware of the existence of vast areas of untapped experience; in fact, one could almost say that the fifteen months spent among the ranks constitute an unwritten masterpiece. Krige acquired a profound respect for the English character, not as encountered among the officers but as revealed by the men. The fortitude and humor, often under conditions of grinding strain, seemed to him inexhaustible. As one of the best-educated men in the camp, his main contribution to its life took the form of a daily newspaper. His program occupied him for the whole day. At about midday he would acquire five or six Italian daily papers. Having developed techniques for the detecting of slant and falsification, he then assembled the news and dictated it to two or three secretaries. He followed the news with comment and interpretation, and the handwritten news-sheets were finally distributed at five o'clock. Apart from its considerable effect in maintaining morale, this newspaper seems to have attained quite a remarkable standard of efficiency. Despite Italian propaganda, it predicted, for instance, at the darkest moment of the war that Stalingrad would not fall.

Although Krige learned that he had been threatened in a broadcast directed at South Africa by "Zeesen" because of his antipropaganda activities in 1940, he was not molested; and he continued to read omnivorously. Both during that period and later, after his officer's status had been restored to him, he studied Leopardi and Dante; and he developed considerably his critical faculties. Even after he was no longer editing the camp newspaper, he went on following what he could glean of the international situation.

The loss of North Africa had had a disastrous effect on Italian civilian morale. The king and certain elements in the army, supported by the Socialists, were secretly seeking to extricate Italy from the war; and when on July 14, provoked by the fall of Sicily and by the bombing of Rome, the cabinet passed a vote of no-confidence in the government, the king arrested Mussolini and asked Badoglio to form a new cabinet. An armistice, coinciding with the landing of the Allies at Brindisi, was announced on September 8. For the prisoners of war, the week that ensued was a crucial one. On the tenth, the Camp Commander informed them that they were free to do as they pleased; on the next day they received radio instructions to remain in camp until liberated by the Allied advance; the day after that, learning that German troops were in Sulmona, they took to the hills. The Nazis had reacted to the armistice with characteristic promptness; they had occupied Rome, set up a Fascist-Republican government in the north, and were preparing to resist with all the skill and tenacity at their command.

The story of the next two months is contained in his magnificent piece of autobiography, *The Way Out,* which describes his six-week march through enemy territory from Sulmona to the Allied line in Campobasso, sixty miles to the south. This book has been called, with justice, one of the finest escape stories of World War II. There have been narratives that are more ingenious, more spectacular, and more brutal; but none has been written with a greater depth of truth and range of sympathy. *The Way Out* is at once a subtle exposition of the mind and feelings of men on the run and a haunting evocation of the pastoral landscape of Ovid and Horace; periods of danger and fear, behind which lay the constant menace of war, alternate with pictures of the splendor of the Abruzzi Mountains or the beauty of autumn forests. But it is in the celebration of the warmth and strength of the Italian peasants, who repeatedly risked their lives for the sake of the fugitives, from nothing but a sense of fundamental human loyalty, that the book's power must finally reside. And out of the encounter between Uys Krige's generous gratitude and their ancient simplicity grows a moving affirmation of all those common bonds that link human beings together, whatever their disputes and differences.

The strange paradox, frequently if unconsciously reflected in such narratives, that to gain freedom is to lose it, found a new and powerful expression when Krige attained his goal. His first contact with liberty took the form of disenchantment. The atmosphere of smugness in the face of indiscriminate destruction, the self-righteous tone of Allied newspapers and publications, the imperturbable racial and social superiority of the officers, and above all the contempt of some of his fellow prisoners for the peasants to whom they owed their lives—all these struck Krige as an intolerable outrage. It was with a feverish sense of urgency, therefore, that, on his return to South Africa a month later, he began to dictate *The Way Out* to his wife. He hoped, perhaps naïvely, that quick publication would affect the attitudes of the Allied High Command. By July, 1944, 250,000 words had been written; revision cut these to 150,000; but publication was delayed till December, 1946, when the book won a belated, if enthusiastic, reception in London.

V   *Return to Europe*

By August, 1946, Krige was back in Cairo; and, with the rank of captain, he accompanied a team of observers to Rome. Appalled at what the war had done to Italy—the invasion had moved like a ploughshare up the three main roads of the peninsula—he collected a truckload of food and clothes to take to his friends at Sulmona. An indescribable reunion took place, of which only one detail, illustrating the fate of an author's manuscripts in time of war, can be mentioned. A bundle of poems and short stories which he had left on the mountain-side on the night of his original escape, and which had been retrieved by a Jewish fellow-prisoner some weeks later while they were still hiding near Sulmona, had been entrusted to their Italian host when they were about to start on their final march south. When news leaked out that this Italian possessed documents belonging to an enemy war-correspondent, two German officers searched his house, but were distracted from their task before they could reach the bedroom in which the papers were concealed. To avoid further risk, the Italian sealed them in a bottle and lowered it down his garden well. There they had remained until the liberation of Sulmona. These manuscripts contained, among other items, the short story "Death of a Zulu" and the poems published in *Hart Sonder Hawe*.

Of the next fifteen months in Europe, during which Uys Krige witnessed the concluding phase of the war and found himself the victim or the hero of a multitude of adventures, only the most cursory account can be given. After a fortnight in liberated Paris, when he met such writers and actors as Camus, Aragon, Dullin and Barrault, he went to London to be trained by the British Broadcasting Corporation in order to follow as a commentator the South African Brigade in its breakthrough to Amsterdam. After a short period of broadcasting in four languages, he was inexplicably recalled to Cairo. He had, a few months previously, received news of the birth of his son Taillefer; he now met his wife and his sister who had brought a touring company of players from South Africa to entertain the troops. Appointed as conducting officer, he travelled with them to Italy and to Austria. He returned to South Africa in March, 1946.

Krige's war experience can be considered, with his first visit to Europe, one of the two central episodes of his life. In 1931, he had discovered the great cultural achievement of Europe; in 1940, he participated in its agony. What he saw and felt in the course of these years left an indelible impression on his mind. It has inspired the themes of a substantial proportion of the work produced since 1945. Indirectly, it had a more profound and extended influence: he had acquired a new wisdom, a fresh understanding, and a greater breadth of humanity. At the age of thirty-five, he was ready for the period of creativity that lay ahead.

CHAPTER 4

The Creative Years

ALTHOUGH no single episode as important as Uys Krige's first visit to Europe or his involvement in the Second World War has occurred since 1945, the last twenty years have been singularly varied and rich, not only in external incident but in inner adventurousness. He continued to travel, first returning to Europe for a period of two years, then later spending seven months in the United States, and a further four months in Europe; he emerged as a first-rate lecturer, broadcaster, and reader of poetry; he began to involve himself in the theater and the production of plays; he continued to participate in public affairs, never wavering in his opposition to racialism and authoritarianism; and, most important of course, he wrote his finest work, not only in his chosen fields of the poetry and the play, but in a department which he has made peculiarly his own, translation, and in the less creative but still exacting discipline of criticism.

When one surveys the period as a whole, one is perhaps most struck by one feature—his capacity for steady development. This capacity will be discussed in far greater detail in the second part of this study, but one may observe here that, without exception, every department of his work has improved with age and experience. At the present moment, though in his fifties, Krige is far from having exhausted the resources of his talent and from settling down to reap the satisfaction of past achievement; he is eagerly looking into the future and preparing himself for better and more sustained creative efforts. "The critics have called me a 'dertiger,'" he says, referring to the literary movement of the 1930's in which he has sometimes been pigeon-holed; "but I consider myself a 'tagtiger'!" By this statement he implies not only that he belongs to some nebulous literary category of the future—the 1980's—which would incidentally correspond to the 1880's, a decade which saw the flowering of modern Dutch poetry, but also that he will be "coming down the straight," as he puts it, precisely at the moment when he enters the threshold of extreme old age. This remark cannot be dismissed as mere irreverence: it is provoked by his sense of growing power.

This capacity for growth, of course, is not accidental or arbitrary. Unlike many writers of prominence he has not squandered his talent but safeguarded it by the exercise of two virtues, the lack of which often leads to self-destruction: honesty and humility. One is struck at once, in meeting him, by the fact that he is a man who tells the truth, not only to himself but also to others; one is also struck by his sense of proportion and his modesty, a quality which has cost him dear in the superficial respect conferred by the world.

As the work accomplished during the post-war years is the central episode in his biography, the last part of this narrative will no longer follow a direct chronological line, but will occasionally anticipate or digress.

I 1946–1950

Uys Krige lived in Johannesburg from 1946 to 1950. During these four and a half years, he published a great backlog of work —his habit of endlessly rewriting and revising has made him an extremely reluctant publisher—*Sol y Sombra* (1948), *Hart Sonder Hawe* (1949), *Vir die Luit en die Kitaar* (For the Lute and the Guitar [1950])—a collection of translations from European poetry mainly written during the 1930's—and *Ver in die Wêreld* (Far in the World [1951]). The advantages of his almost obsessional concern for polishing a text is perhaps best illustrated by the career of *The Way Out*, the one book, as has been noted, whose publication seemed to him a matter of urgency. The language of the original edition was riddled with the faults typical of someone writing in a second language: clumsiness of phrase, both rhythmic and verbal; overwriting; and a reliance on the hackneyed expression. He therefore launched himself into a program of correction that was to last off and on for eight years. As he says in his preface to the third edition (1955): "For ten years now there has been for me no escape from *The Way Out*. At last I can say: 'It's done, conscience, and I can do no more about it.'" This heroic act of revision may indeed have cost him a decade, but it taught him English. Without it, one would not have *The Dream and the Desert* and the translation of five of his plays. He has achieved the very rare distinction of being a bilingual writer, even though his Afrikaans is superior in every respect to his English.

His first original work after his return from the war consisted in three one-act plays written in quick succession: *Die Grootkannonne* (The Great Cannons), *Die Sluipskutter* (The Sniper), and *Alle Paaie Gaan na Rome* (All Roads Lead to Rome). It seems that in this outburst he was exorcising, as it were, his recent experience: all three are concerned with some aspect of World War II. Three years later, he was translating *The Way Out* into Afrikaans, a task completed two years later; but this work has still not found its way to the public. Since then, except for a recent full-length play still in manuscript form, he has not directly concerned himself with the theme of war.

Meanwhile, he had thrown himself into a multitude of other activities, all related to literature. His arrival in Johannesburg seems to have occasioned a sustained demand for public lectures on a variety of subjects matched only by the variety of audience. He spoke on the war to the general public, on literature to the university, and on politics to the city. To quote one example of his involvement in political and public affairs: in 1946 occurred certain disturbances in Johannesburg. A number of African trade unions, which were shortly to be banned, had grown steadily in numbers and power during the war; in August the strongest of these, the African Mineworkers' Union, went on strike over the question of wages. Socialist in complexion, and not recognized by the authorities, the union decided its sole method of negotiation was to show its members in the streets; and when, therefore, seventy thousand of them marched to the City Hall, large police contingents drove them back to their locations.

At this point, Uys Krige joined a committee of distinguished liberals to assist the distressed and to present their cause. He also began to appear frequently on radio programs; for instance, he participated in a national brains trust in the company of such writers and journalists as Nicholas Monsarrat and Colin Legum. At that time, he also had a brief association with the cinema, providing text and poetry for a Shell documentary *Salute to the Voortrekkers,* which subsequently was shown in all parts of the world.

But his most important venture was his attempt to establish, with the assistance of a friend, Erhard Planje, a literary review called *Vandag* (Today).

Vandag represented an act of faith in the future of South African writing—English, as well as Afrikaans. Although only four numbers were produced—both advertisements and organization were deficient—it achieved, by South African standards, real distinction. Some of the earliest prose of Nadine Gordimer, the poetry of Guy Butler and Antony Delius, as well as the work of Roy Campbell, William Plomer, Uys Krige, Alan Paton, Olga Kirsch, Christina van Heyningen, Herman Bosman, and Van Melle, appeared in its pages.

One may disagree with Uys Krige's evaluation of the work of individual authors, but, on basic critical standards, he seems to have been absolutely sound. By the phrase "South African writing," for instance, he did not imply anything beyond "writing produced in South Africa." The relationship between the literature of the new country and that of the so-called "mother country" is often an uneasy one. When a new literature, anxious to liberate itself from the great parent tradition in order to achieve independence and distinctiveness, deliberately produces work that is different, it usually loses all originality and universality. This truth Uys Krige has never ignored. In a lecture given in Johannesburg some years later, he puts the point firmly: "Our writing can be as characteristic or typical as it likes, but if it has no universal values, it has no deep human truth, if its human content cannot at the same time apply to any other country under the sun, its peculiar flavor, its savor or *goût de terroir* or *sabor castizo* as the Spaniards say, falls more in the domain of folklore than of literature." [1] At the deepest level, the phrase "a national literature" would seem to be a contradiction in terms.

II   *1950*

In February, 1950, he settled—this time permanently—in the Cape, where he eventually acquired two domiciles: one at Clifton, a Cape Town suburb under Lion's Head; the other at Onrust, a small seaside village about sixty miles to the east of the city. This move was provoked partly by a desire to return to the land of his childhood, partly to find a theatrical milieu more congenial to his wife than Johannesburg had been. Both these motives are reflected in the work which then began to engage his attention. He put the finishing touches to a three-act play, *Die Twee Lampe* (The Two Lamps), originally written in Johannesburg in 1948—a tragedy set in the landscape of his early childhood—and followed it with what became his most successful comedy, *Die Ryk Weduwee* (The Rich Widow), a work steeped in the language and atmosphere of the Western Province. Produced by the National Theatre Organization, it was at first damned with faint praise by the Afrikaans newspapers, but it was a success from the start and toured the country for eleven months, ultimately netting £24,000.

At this time, Krige was also translating steadily, particularly from modern French and Spanish poetry. He had also acquired a working knowledge of Portuguese and was studying the work of the Brazilian poets, especially Manuel Bandeira, Murilo Mendes, and Jorge de Lima; and he noted the way in which they had absorbed and transformed the traditions of Europe: "They made all (or almost all) Surrealism's discoveries their own, truly assimilated them, adding their own vigor, emotional warmth, intuitional power and surging movement to arrive at a new synthesis, and a new poetry that is both modern and their own." [2] Again, Afrikaans versions of the lyrics of the Spanish Americans, often accompanied by introductory essays, appeared regularly in the pages of Cape Town periodicals and magazines: the Mexican Martinez, the Chilian Gabriela Mistral, Vicente Huidobro and Pablo Neruda, the Peruvian Cesar Vallejo, and the Cuban Nicolas Guillen. It is scarcely surprising that Krige was asked, when visiting Yale University, to lecture, not on South African, but on South American poetry!

He also worked on French poetry, translating the appealing verses of Jacques Prévert and, above all, the poems of surrealist Paul Eluard. Fourteen years later, a selection of the latter's work, with page by page Afrikaans translations, appeared in book form. As this book represents his most sustained effort in the translation of the work of a single author, who, what is more, is at the center of a movement that has had a great influence on Spanish and Latin American literary circles and which has always greatly interested Uys Krige himself, it is necessary to devote a few lines to it. It is introduced by a sixty-page discussion of the Surrealist movement that cannot but earn admiration for its clarity, for Surrealism is not a subject that easily lends itself to coherent summary. The theology of its archpriest, André Breton, is at the very least indigestible; and far too much of its poetry seems to be composed on the principle of a submental association of ideas. Its keyword "liberty" is often the excuse for mere anarchy; and its stress on such concepts as "the subconscious," "the dream," "the vision," etc., is frequently little more than gibberish. However, one can say in its favor that the Surrealist movement led to the clearing away of a great deal of academic humbug and bourgeois narrowness and, more significantly, to the writing of a poetry that has strange simplicity and great evocative power.

Uys Krige's introduction deals with both these qualities in an admirably lucid and lively way, and his selection of Eluard's poetry represents what is best in the movement itself. Eluard's revolt against the academies—what the Brazilians have called "the Bastilles of reaction"—is part of his rejection of snobbery and privilege. His Communism is not doctrinaire but seems to grow out of a deep feeling for ordinary life acquired through his experience of the suffering of three wars. There is indeed a great deal in Eluard that Uys Krige would find congenial: his participation in the French Resistance, his faith in man, and the spontaneity and simplicity of his poetry. One is not surprised, therefore, to find that Krige's translations give the impression of having effortlessly "happened."

III   A Poet's Values

Although Uys Krige is, like every South African, profoundly affected by the local political scene, his commitment is that of a poet, not a politician. In spite of the fact that he has, throughout his life, resolutely opposed all forms of oppression and seems to be temperamentally a radical rather than a conservative; he is not an active member of any South African political party. He has said, in a recent address at the University of Natal, that, while it is essential for a poet to keep out of politics if he is to write true poetry, it is sometimes necessary for him to return to politics if he is to continue writing at all. A poet's work grows out of his values, not out of the policies of his party. But if, by his detachment and silence, he finds himself acquiescing in what he knows to be wrong, he may begin to undermine the integrity of his values; and, in so doing, he exhausts the very sources of his talent. This kind of commitment is admirably exemplified in Uys Krige's attitude to the disenfranchisement of the Colored people—the million and three-quarters South Africans of mixed race—and so deserves some attention.

When Dr. Malan swept his Nationalist party to victory in 1948, he quickly realized that the presence of nearly forty-five thousand antagonistic votes on the same roll as that of the white electorate constituted a permanent threat to his security. He therefore determined to relegate the Colored voters to a separate roll, allowing them only token representation; but he was hindered by the fact that the rights of the Colored were entrenched in the Constitution. His attempts to bypass the Constitution were attacked by the courts and by a large proportion of the population of South Africa, notably by an ex-servicemen's organization known as the "Torch Commando." Uys Krige, who had himself been alarmed by the growth of arbitrariness in public affairs, embraced the cause of the Colored people with a conviction strengthened by his frequent contact with them and by his admiration for their vitality and courage, the charm of the devil-may-care way of life of many of them, and their idiomatic use of vernacular Afrikaans (see Appendix). In 1951, Krige participated in a "Torch-Commando" campaign and spoke to crowds numbering from twenty-two thousand in Port Elizabeth to fifty thousand in Cape Town.

Such opposition forced Dr. Malan to withdraw, and it was only in 1955 that his successor, J. G. Strijdom, artificially enlarged the Senate to give the Nationalists the required majority. Uys Krige's concern for the fate of the Colored people moved him profoundly. A year later, he said in Johannesburg: "We are completely shut off from this teeming hinterland of real *volkslewe*, from all the pullulating life of our working classes. We do not know it intimately, what it feels like, tastes like, sounds like, smells like." And he adds appositely enough, "To write really well about a thing, I feel you should know it so well that you do not think about it any more, you've almost forgotten about it, it has become part of you, part of your blood-stream, as it were. We Europeans are a mighty long way from this in our knowledge of our African or Coloured fellow-citizens." [3] He, however, was not such a long way from this form of instinctive knowledge. In 1957, strengthened by the thought of how Lorca had written about the gypsies, he was composing a magnificent collection of lyrical-dramatic ballads celebrating the joys and sorrows of the Colored people. These were finally published in 1960, under the title *Ballade van die Groot Begeer* (Ballad of the Great Desiring), and remain his best poetry to date.

IV *Europe Again*

At the end of March, 1952, he took advantage of a bursary offered to him by the French government in recognition of his services to French culture in South Africa (apart from his translations, he had been president of the Alliance Française in Johannesburg from 1947 to 1949). He spent the first nine months in London where he studied the modern British theater—which, incidentally, he claimed to be in a state of decadence because of its antiheroic prejudices and its reduction of dialogue—and finished writing the English short stories published under the title *The Dream and the Desert*. This book was acclaimed both in England and in America. *Time Magazine,* for instance, called it "as good a book of short stories as is current in the English language"; such newspapers as the *New York Herald Tribune,* the *New York Times* and the (then) *Manchester Guardian* gave it prominent and enthusiastic coverage.

In December, 1952, he went to Paris where, under the patronage of the French government and writers like Gabriel Marcel, he became a guest of the Comédie Française, and was introduced to many distinguished personalities of the Parisian theatrical and literary world. For the first time he got to know the metropolis which had given birth, through Baudelaire, to the poetry of the city so characteristic of modern writing. He spent much of the winter attending plays and wandering on the banks of the Seine and visiting its historic districts where, as he says, "the sadness sweats from the stones." After a month spent in Holland and Flanders—countries in which he has acquired a real reputation—he set off on a pilgrimage to post Civil-War Spain. He revisited many of his old haunts—Barcelona, for instance, seemed strangely to lack its old Catalan spirit—for he had many ghosts to lay. He gave lectures on South African and Spanish poetry on the occa-

sion of the eight hundredth anniversary of the University of Sala-
manca, and he again got to know several fellow writers of international repute.

On his second visit to Spain an artistic incident occurred of major importance. Several years before, in conversation with a Portuguese friend, Krige had learned an ancient Iberian legend in
which an old woman had acquired the magical power to fasten to
an orange tree anyone who touched it; she had in this way ren-
dered ineffective the figure of Death who had come to fetch her
but with sinister long-term effects on the village community. That
this theme had long interested Uys Krige can be seen from the
fact that he had already told the legend twice in the form of short
stories.[4] Plunged in the vivid life of Spain which recalled so
strongly his early carefree days, he suddenly felt inspired to dram-
atize the legend. He accordingly spent three months in Tossa del
Mar, a fishing village on the Costa Brava, living in the house of an
old fisherman's wife.

This period has been delightfully evoked in two essays published in *Sout van die Aarde:* "Senora Adela" and "My drie
Kyfagtige Katalane" (My Three Quarrelsome Catalans). These
essays describe the magnificent house and the centuries-old village in which he worked and which became the setting for his
play, and also some of the people, illiterate but rich and poetic in
their speech, with whom he came into daily contact, and who, as
it turned out, unobtrusively invited themselves into the play.
There is some justification for claiming that these three enchanted
months, when he spent the day composing what some of his
readers have claimed to be the finest play in Afrikaans, and the
evenings talking to the local fishing-folk, with the fragrance of the
orange harvest outside and with the sound of the Mediterranean
in the distance, were perhaps among the happiest of his life.

V *Play Production*

Returned to Cape Town in March, 1954, he could look back on
this latest episode in what he has called his "love affair with Europe" with satisfaction. He had originally witnessed the destruction of Europe; he had now participated in its recovery. His stay
in London and particularly in Paris had enormously enlarged his
understanding of producing and acting for the stage. He had re-

explored the art galleries of Britain, Belgium, Holland, France, and Spain—he has always had a special partiality for the visual arts, and his own descriptive powers are evidence enough of the keenness of his eye. Finally, he had come into enriching contact with a large number of poets, philosophers, and actors of international standing. He has said himself that these two years allowed him to assimilate and digest much of what he had felt fragmentarily during the war: emotionally, they seem to have been an integrative experience.

His newly acquired interest in play production became at once evident. His friendship with Cape Town producer Pietro Nolte resulted in the creation of an experimental theater company, the activities of which absorbed him during the following two years to the exclusion of practically everything else. In his wife, Lydia Lindeque, the company possessed an actress of substance and reputation, and the plays produced by Nolte—Lorca's *Yerma,* Euripides' *Medea,* and Goldoni's *La Locandiera* (under the title *Mirandolina*)—are sufficient evidence of the range of her talent. Uys Krige's role in this venture was largely confined to literary matters. He suggested the three plays to Nolte; introduced and supported them with lectures, articles and broadcasts, widely extending his acquaintance with the great tradition of classic plays; he revised and improved the English translations of *Yerma,* the choruses of which he entirely rewrote; and he assisted the producer on general questions of interpretation and presentation.

It was then, too, that he strengthened another aspect of his talent, the public reading of poetry. Uys Krige has sometimes said of himself that he is an "acteur manqué," and anyone who has heard him read—particularly in Afrikaans, for his English accent is not perfect—is bound to agree. His mobile and expressive face, his compelling, high-toned voice, and the ease and variety of his gestures are all arresting. But what is most notable about his recitals —if such a term can be applied to a performance that is nothing if not spontaneous—is his truly masterly control of rhythm. He can give a poem such a sweep and cadence that to hear him recite something one knows is to re-experience it in all its original freshness and excitement. He has in fact evolved a technique in presenting his own and others' poetry that is quite individual.

His lectures, which he modestly calls "personal chats," are a fluent mingling of reminiscence, critical insight, erudition, playful wit, and full-blooded recitation. It is inevitable that such an approach should occasionally falter, for it depends for its success on a strong sense of audience and on ebullience of personality; and such factors, in turn, depend on mood and inspiration. But the response of his audiences is usually memorable, and his auditors come away enlivened with a new sense of the importance of people and of poetry. There is something of the ballad-monger about him—a great wanderer, he is equally at ease with a simple country audience or a sophisticated university assembly—and those who describe him, after one of his lectures, as a contemporary troubadour are not romanticizing.

Die Goue Kring was produced twice during that period—first in Johannesburg as part of the commemoration of that city's seventieth anniversary and later in Cape Town—after Nolte and his company had been forced to discontinue through lack of support. This second performance, this time by amateurs, and enhanced by the music of Gilberto Bonegio, was very favorably received by press and public alike.

Since then, Krige's interest in theater has shown no signs of abating: three further plays have come from his pen: two translations, *Yerma* (1963) and *Twelfth Night* (at the moment enjoying a triumphant run in the Transvaal), and an original full-length comedy on a war theme, *Die Loodswaaiers* (The Leadswingers), which is still in manuscript form. The two translations, which are equally magnificent (the Dutch critic Ben van Eysselsteyn, for instance, has called his *Yerma* "a sublime translation"), are briefly discussed in the last chapter of this study. The *Yerma* publication, however, contains a forty-five page essay on Lorca and the European dramatic tradition which cannot be ignored. The essay as a whole clearly reveals his attitude to the play as an art form. It can be summarized briefly under four headings: (a) an emphasis on simplicity and clarity of structure; (b) a mistrust of "intellectualism"—whether in the form of abstract language or the propounding of a thesis; (c) the conviction that the play's proper concern is individual character; and (d) a belief in the fundamentally poetic nature of drama. This point of view may not be startlingly original; but, anchored as it is in a love for the great plays of the past, it remains admirably sane and central. It has not only sharpened his insight into the inanities and pretensions of contemporary dra-

matic movements but has strengthened the human relevance of
his own work.

However far it ranges, though, this essay is fundamentally concerned with Lorca, a poet in whom Krige has found inspiration
for over thirty years and to whom he owes two great translations.
One may therefore take this opportunity to summarize briefly the
nature of his relationship with the great Spanish poet. A point that
must be made at the outset is the astonishingly high standard of
the Afrikaans versions of *Yerma* and the *Lament* for the bullfighter. They are infinitely superior to any English or French versions I have seen; and, leaving aside the quality of Uys Krige's
talent, two factors can be advanced to explain this success: the
nature of Afrikaans society, and the temperament of Uys Krige.
Many Afrikaners possess an unsophisticated simplicity not incom-
patible with the elemental, passionate nature of Lorca's characters. This society is, like that of Spain, still largely agrarian, puri-
tanical, and, in some ways, even primitive. Finally, the landscape
of South Africa, which, naturally, is reflected in Afrikaans in all
sorts of subtle ways, is strangely reminiscent of the Spanish countryside.

As for Uys Krige himself, his attraction to Lorca was immediate
and permanent. He found in him a sensuous lyricism, a boldness
of image, a richness of texture and music, and an intensity of feeling which were at once congenial. Krige also, as his own work
shows, found himself drawn to Lorca's skill and subtlety in the use
of contrast; and in a portion of his essay he analyzes this principle
in *Yerma* with the confidence of a connoisseur. Last, but not least,
he discovered a playwright who was also a poet—an author
whose lyrics were also dramatic. All this may perhaps explain why
Lorca found, in Uys Krige, his most memorable translator.

VI *Study in America*

It was Uys Krige's interest in drama which earned him a Carnegie grant to study the American theater. Having received in April,
1958, an honorary doctorate from the University of Natal—where
he delivered a series of stirring lectures for which he is still
remembered—he arrived in New York in March, 1959, and spent
some time on the East Coast, particularly at Yale and at Harvard.

He then visited California and the South, and at The University of Texas (Austin) he gave a course of lectures and seminars on Commonwealth literature. He attended several conferences, notably a nation-wide congress of writers, critics and translators sponsored by the Ford Foundation at Washington; there he met such representatives of American culture as Robert Lowell, Aaron Copland, and Richard Eberhart.

Uys Krige has always had great admiration for modern American literature. In a lecture delivered in Johannesburg some years before and entitled, significantly enough, "Has Africa, Like America, a Characteristic Contribution to make to Literature?" he said: "There are two things especially remarkable for me about America's valuable contribution to world literature. The first and perhaps the most important one is its democratic feeling for life. Already, early in the second half of the nineteenth century, it had cut right through the class barrier, delivering English literature from a class-bound consciousness as rigid as it was inhibiting. . . . America's second great contribution to modern literature is the richness, variety and racy strength of its dialogue—whether it comes straight off a Brooklyn street, out of the Californian cotton-picker's cottage, the Chicago tenement slum, the San Francisco honky tonk, the Texan ranch house or the artist's dive in Greenwich Village." [5] Krige's visit to the United States was, therefore, scarcely that of the detached tourist: to come in contact with the physical presence of the country was to enlarge a relationship already long established. And his contact with the people was intimate and natural. When asked, for instance, about his experiences in the United States, he answered that one of his achievements there was to sit for two and a half hours next to Marilyn Monroe in the Actor's Studio in New York. Without recognizing her, he thought, in his innocence, that she was some vague South African actress he had met before!

But it seems that, in certain respects, he was finally a little disturbed by his experience of the United States. In an interview given to the liberal newspaper *Contact* on his return to South Africa, he spoke of the isolation of American writers from one another and, because of their criticism of American life, from other Americans. Of the so-called "American Dilemma," he said: "It is not the American dilemma at all, of course. It's the dilemma of modern man at his most industrialised and with the maximum of

possessions. The American *is* modern man, not just an American."
He added, however, "There is so much vitality and genuine ideal-
ism in America that whatever flaws and faults their pattern—their
way of life—may have, I feel their faults are only part of a transi-
tional phase. . . . If you believe in people, as I do, then you believe in Americans." [6]

VII *The 1960's*

In November 1959, he was back in Europe to join his daughter
Eulalia in a trip through France, Italy, and Greece. It was his first
visit to the latter country, and an unforgettable one. Back in South
Africa at the beginning of 1960, he settled down in Cape Town to
a virtually unbroken period of work; and he has not been out of
the country since.[7]

The last four or five years have, in fact, been astonishingly pro-
ductive. The year 1960 saw the publication of *Ballade van die
Groot Begeer* and of his selection of the poetry of Roy Campbell;
1961, *Sout van die Aarde* and a definitive edition of his poems
from 1927 to 1940; 1962, *Yerma* and the English version of his one-
act plays; 1963, his translation of Eluard and *The Two Lamps*. He
has, in addition to these publications, several works ready, or virtually ready, for publication: two volumes of poetry, at least four
volumes of essays, three volumes of translation from French and
Latin American poetry, two full-length plays, the translations of
Twelfth Night and of Moliere's *Le Medecin Malgré Lui*, and the
Afrikaans version of *The Way Out*. This work has been aug-
mented by countless radio broadcasts, public lectures, and newspaper articles; by a continued involvement in the theater; and by
fearless criticism of governmental autocracy in various fields: the
undermining of university autonomy, the censorship of the press,
and official interference in the work of artists and writers. For
example, in the celebrated blasphemy case of 1953, when a young
Johannesburg painter was arraigned on grounds of religious irreverence, Krige spent three days in the witness box providing evidence in favor of the defense.

Apart from the new depth and assurance in Krige's recent work,
the last few years are notable for his emergence as a bilingual
writer. There is no question but that his touch in Afrikaans is both
surer and more original; and, in his tendency to translate his origi-

nal works from one language to another, one may sometimes deplore the fact that his energy is not more regularly diverted into new work. But this tendency shows a need to try to find an audience both larger, and perhaps more sympathetic, than the relatively small local public. Besides, to a person as sensitive to current political directions as Uys Krige, the question of the survival of Afrikaans may occasionally and uneasily raise its head.

In fact, Uys Krige's position as a writer—despite his popularity with a large proportion of the common people and despite the sincere respect and admiration which he has earned from many critics of taste and judgment—has remained, in his own country at least, strangely uncertain and ambiguous. He writes, in an atmosphere not very propitious to literature. Indeed, on this subject, he has spoken frequently and passionately: as recently as June, 1964, he explained to a Durban audience the crippling effect of perpetual censorship—not only of an author's published work but, more significantly, of his unwritten books—because of the way the unconscious levels of his creative mind might be affected.

Again, he has, to quite a surprising degree, been the victim of the silent disregard and of the invisible contempt which he seems to have earned from the Nationalist Party since 1939. His fierce sense of independence which is part, as he himself asserts, of the inherited traditions of the Voortrekkers, and his deep and natural sense of humanity, have made it impossible for him to cooperate with unprincipled authoritarianism in any of its forms, whether as a repressive party machine or as a phalanx of critical pundits.[8] But he, like others before him, has earned his punishment for not conforming, as a single example will show. It is an almost inconceivable fact that a man whose work has received enthusiastic praise from such cultural centers as Belgium, Holland, England, and the United States, and who has steadily produced an impressive quantity of serious work for over thirty-five years, has not been awarded the Hertzog Prize in any of the three categories of prose, poetry, and drama—an annual literary award by the highest literary body in the country, the South African Academy.

This almost systematic program of discrimination has not been without its adverse effects on him, but the fact that Uys Krige, far from succumbing to discouragement or bitterness, has improved his work, both in variety and importance, with every passing year, is an astonishing reflection on his moral and artistic quality.

He is now in his mid-fifties and at the peak of his powers. As this all too brief survey of his life has tried to show, his talent has found expression in many fields, and not least in his capacity for living. It is impossible, of course, to predict what his future work will be like; but this at least can be said: he will certainly continue to enrich both the language in which he writes, and the humanity of those who can see him for what he is—a poet whose work is deeply rooted in the central virtues of generosity, courage, and truthfulness.

PART II

Critical

CHAPTER 5

The One-Act Plays

I The Slighter Ones

BEING a born poet with a good deal of dramatic sense, Uys Krige has for many years been interested in playwriting. His best plays are his full-length ones, which will be discussed in the next chapter. This chapter is devoted to his very early and fairly early experiments in drama in which his best powers are not shown, for these plays are all in that rather uneasy form, the one-acter. It is very difficult for a writer to sail anything but a mere skiff of a play on the shallow quantity of time allowed to the one-acter, and most of the plays discussed in this chapter are very slight works; all are of some merit, but only two or three of them are outstanding.

The slightest of all is the radio-play *Die Gees van die Water* (The Spirit of the Water), written in 1937. Of plot, there is virtually none; and the play is undistinguished except for the wealth and flexibility of its language. *Die Ongeskrewe Stuk* (The Unwritten Piece [1939]) is an experiment in audience-participation, and the whole play is made to appear completely impromptu. A producer has been promised a play by Uys Krige—the piece hasn't arrived; so he decides to entertain single-handed the audience with recitations and songs and so on. But he keeps being thwarted before he has even begun. First, the curtain has gone up without his noticing it and has stuck, exposing him to the audience while he is arguing with the pianist who won't get off the stage because the actors haven't come yet. Then a "student of drama" rises from the audience and pontificates about how a theater must be treated with reverence, like a cathedral; next a drunken actor from the balcony yells to the producer to come out and have a beer with him; then two girls from the floor rave about plays not having to be written but simply to be "made out of Life," and so on and so on. At last the producer gives up and consents to go out for the beer; elated, everybody shouts from the wings, "Long live Life." Someone cries, "To Hell with construction!"; and then an excited voice calls out "It's working! It's working!" And, sticking from time to time, the curtain slowly descends.

Though this experiment certainly proves that to say "To Hell with construction!" is to take the backbone out of a play and leave it sprawling invertebrate in all directions—and therefore some portions of it drag—on the whole the play does achieve the spontaneity aimed at. And it so dances and sparkles with fun and humor that one can temporarily join in at the end with the Musician, who cries, rejoicing: "Happiness, people! I feel dotty, dizzy, drunk with it! [Joyously] Long live the Drama! Long live Love! Long live Life!" There is a great deal of comic movement in the piece and parts of it must be delightful to see. But Aristotle is right: a play depends for its life on the development of the central action, where everything in the play indispensably proceeds from and leads to something else in it; for one is left at the end of this play, in spite of much enjoyment, with the feeling that it has all been rather pointless.

Die Skaapwagters van Bethlehem (The Shepherds of Bethlehem), written in 1937, is a simple little nativity play for the radio which has achieved some degree of reality by the way the setting, the characters, and the dialogue of the familiar story are imagined as if found on the South African veld. Uys Krige adds a tragic touch by making the shepherds talk about one Rachel and one or two other pregnant women who are all haunted by a prophetic intuition of the coming Massacre of the Innocents. At the end, the dawning of the star in its extraordinary brilliance is dramatically imagined. Otherwise this little play is not remarkable, for faith in the Christian story is neither present, of course, as it is in the early miracle-play writers, nor is its nature profoundly enough explored for a more skeptical age.

Die Wit Muur (The White Wall [1938]) tells about a lad in the Boer War, who refuses, even on threat of immediate execution, to betray the whereabouts of his father's commando. Suspense mounts painfully towards the end: the execution squad has loaded rifles levelled at the child as he stands trembling with terror but still stubborn against a wall which the first sunlight of the day is illuminating with a brilliant white light. The count for the command to fire is already being made when the British officer in charge gives the order to lower rifles; exclaiming that the boy is "a man, a real man," he catches the swooning youngster in his arms. The play is thin, but the suspense is excellently maintained in the last few minutes of the action and keeps it alive.

Fuente Sagrada (Sacred Spring [1939]) is about the Civil War in Spain. It tells how Marais, a South African volunteer in the government army, happens during a retreat to be entrusted with the task of carrying an extremely heavy box of secret documents to a certain section of the front; he knows that if he fails the whole enterprise, perhaps the whole war, will be lost. The play deals with Marais's attempts to persuade or coerce a peasant farmer to jettison his own most dearly bought belongings and to transport the box in his cart. While this is going on, the entirely peaceful village of Calvario in the distance is bombed by the Fascists and reduced to rubble. Various survivors enter and show in different ways how dreadfully the disaster has affected them. None of these people has any idea what the war is about; the peasant especially is in a state of bottomless ignorance about the political issues. He therefore, even under threat of death, refuses to leave behind the possessions he has slaved for all his life to accommodate the box on his cart. But, when Marais finally makes him understand that he, Marais, and thousands like him have come from the farms of other countries far away to fight for Spain and to help the peasants, he yields; and the audience is left confident that he, Marais, and the box will reach their destination safely.

This play, though not uninteresting or undramatic, is not entirely convincing. One or two of the characters could have been eliminated with advantage. The three insane victims of the bombing, though they are imagined, are not yet deeply enough imagined, so that the play does not sufficiently emerge from the ideas on which it is based into full, convincing, undeniable humanity.

Die Arrestasie (The Arrest) was written in 1939, and first published in 1946. The final version of this play appeared in 1965 in *Skerm en Masker* (Curtain and Mask) by G. Beukes. The action occurs in 1706 in the time of that tyrannical governor of the Cape of Good Hope, Willem Adriaan van der Stel, when a number of farmers—some Hollanders; some Frenchmen, Huguenot refugees from the revocation of the Edict of Nantes; some South African born—banded together to sign a complaint to the Dutch East India Company (then the owners of the Cape) about the despotism of the governor. In the play, the complainants are secretly warned of imminent arrest. The wife of one of them, Cornelia van Zyl, rides to warn the other wives and sweethearts, who are by chance all assembled in one house and whose menfolk have silently disappeared, leaving no inkling of their whereabouts. This last fact, says Cornelia, who knows where the men are, is their best safeguard against cross-examination. But just before the dragoons arrive, the thirteen-year-old son of their Huguenot hostess, Suzanne Seugret du Toit, rushes in; and, before they can stop him, he blurts out where the menfolk are. Hastily they bundle him into a cupboard with cake in it, and hardly have they done so when in comes Captain Hasewinkel with his dragoons. In vain he tries to bully the women into betraying their men. Then the child, who has been gorging himself on the cake, suddenly feels sick and shouts anxiously to be let out of the cupboard. When Hasewinkel, guessing the truth, begins to cross-examine him, the child parries for a while, then gets Hasewinkel to ask him his name. "It is Jean Coligny du Toit," he says ". . . do you know who Coligny was?" At this question Hasewinkel, a stout Protestant himself, is stirred. "I have done my duty as a soldier," he says to the women. "Now as a man I have something to say to you! 'Strenge here, kort regere' [Stern lords, short rule]. Good morning!" And, saluting, he departs.

When I first saw this play many years ago, it struck me as too simply and optimistically heroic. The audience is not forced to imagine, thought I, what might have been the cost of resistance. Consequently, the play is a little facile. But when I saw the play recently, though it was badly done, the texture of it turned out to be so amusing that it struck me as really a comedy of manners. It was the revised version I saw, with its very lively and varied dialogue, rich in comic detail, and revealing with a good deal of entertaining wit and picturesqueness the differences in manners, personality, and national attitudes of the various characters. The emphasis was decidedly on comedy—on gay and lighthearted comedy. It is a pity that the peg on which it is all made to hang is serious without being serious enough, or that it ends not in comedy but in rather too-easy heroics.

II *The Three More Substantial Ones*

Least of these plays is *Die Grootkanonne* of which Krige has
now published an English version called *The Big Shots*. But,
though the play has been improved by some cuts and some
drunken lapses into verse, the dialogue in the Afrikaans version is
much more genuinely that of ex-soldiers than that in the English
one. But *Die Grootkanonne* (literally "The Great Cannons"),
written in 1946, is a big advance on the plays we have discussed
so far.

The plot, however, is slight, and the substance of the play is to
be found in the amusing language, comical movements, and
rather taking characters of the two ex-volunteers from World War
II, Ben and Stoffel, who occupy the stage practically all the time.
They have both been thrown out of a pub at half-past ten, and are
now outside Stoffel's house in Stellenbosch, where Stoffel's newly
married wife Anna lies asleep. They are extremely, ridiculously,
and vociferously drunk; and Ben protests mainly about how in the
war they were Big Shots but are now regarded as merely a pair of
"here, you's." When no efforts can wake Anna, they decide to steal
and to shoot the tiny historical cannon at "the Braak," the old
common nearby. This they do; and a constable, also an ex-soldier,
appears, arrests Stoffel, and begins to lead him off, leaving Ben,
who has for the fifth time lost his footing and is happily lying on
his back singing Italian songs. The sound of someone running
downstairs is heard; the door is unlocked and swings open; Anna,
a very small, pretty woman in a nightgown appears and with a
stout broomstick she fells the constable with a tremendous blow.
In falling, he collides with Stoffel; and the play ends with the
constable on the ground, Stoffel staggering, Ben sitting up humming, and Anna shouting in a deep, musical voice: "Jan Smuts!
Jan Smuts! Bring your whole Force! Your whole Force!"

This outline of the plot gives no idea of how comical the little
farce (it is almost a farce) is. The fun resides partly in the contrast between the appearance of the characters and what they say
and do: Anna is very small and feminine and delicately made,
which makes her strong-arm tactics in dealing with the three men
all the more ludicrous; Stoffel (under her yoke) is a huge blond
man with innocent blue eyes and a contented smile; Ben is about
eight inches shorter, thin, dark, and tremendously lively in the

manner of Western Province people descended from the French. This sharpens the point of such things as Ben's indignation when Stoffel mildly corrects his sentimental reminiscence of how he, Ben, carried the wounded Stoffel "down the mountain at Stanco on my shoulders." "Wait a bit, man," says Stoffel, " . . . wasn't it I who carried you down the mountain on my shoulders?" Upon which Ben retorts with indignation, "When the need was there, the breach was sprung into, a burden was borne, a heavy burden . . . a task was performed to the uttermost . . . that's all. Does it matter who was above and who below? Between comrades that is a trifle. . . ."

Ben is much drunker than Stoffel, and at the same time he is as aggressive as a fighting bantam. The warlike intentions of his movements don't coincide at all with their performance. For example, he gathers himself together with his head forward like a butting ram to charge the constable: "Make way, people, here I come!" he yells; and, as he charges, he roars: "I'll flatten you, you scoundrel, as we flattened them on the top of the mountain!" He "dives at the constable's hip like a rugby three-quarter about to bring down his opponent." The constable, unmoved, "very slightly swings his free arm, and Ben lies stretched out full-length on the ground."

Though the play might have more impact if cut a little, it is packed with lively language. The two men are so blissfully elated with drink, so happily sentimental, and Ben is so eloquently boastful, in a voluble flow of vivid language, about Italy and the war. There are a couple of more serious, even pathetic passages; one is about the women to whom Ben has become attached in Italy; in the other, the comrades poignantly recall their partisan friend Antonio, who "came sailing over the clods like a snake" in a hail of bullets to save them when they were in danger. These passages also give an idea of the pleasure deeper than suffering—or than intoxication—that the men got from comradeship. The play is nearly all comic, however, in an Afrikaans copiously varied. Krige does not hesitate to interpose sentences of English or High Dutch to add a satiric effect. For example, "Love locked out!" cries Ben in English when he and his besotted, henpecked husband of a friend find the door locked. "Love locked out!" And "Ik het gezegd" (I have spoken) they say with Caesar-like dignity, in

High Dutch, after a declaration. Altogether, plot, movements, and language are charged with high spirits.

The last two one-act plays, *Die Sluipskutter* (The Sniper) and *Alle Paaie Gaan na Rome* (All Roads Lead to Rome), both of which have been translated into English by Uys Krige, go deeper than any that have preceded them. *Die Sluipskutter* (1946) happens on a plain in Italy towards the very end of the last war—in April, 1945. The curtain goes up on a German soldier, Heinrich, bent over a rock with his gun levelled; near him a young South African sergeant in a brand-new uniform lies dead on the ground. Two South African soldiers enter silently behind him—Captain Meyer (who one learns later is a German-Jewish refugee) and Sergeant Boshoff. Though Heinrich has no chance, he will not at first surrender because the order has gone out from headquarters that, since the Allies shoot all their prisoners, German soldiers must fight to the death. On being reassured, he gives in. He has stayed behind after all the other Germans have fled, partly because his feet are in a dreadful condition and partly to protect his lieutenant, who is badly wounded. He admits that he killed the young South African sergeant: he had turned to see the South African aiming at him; they had pulled their triggers simultaneously, and the South African had missed.

Meyer and Boshoff recognize the corpse as that of Liebenberg, whose twenty-first birthday it is; and they remark upon how stricken their colonel will be, for he hates to lose any of his men, and he is extremely attached to this particular boy, whose godfather he is. In fact, Colonel Venter has been so incensed by the way snipers have lately picked off—cruelly and quite senselessly since the outcome of the struggle is now beyond all doubt—more than a dozen of his men that he has sworn to shoot the next sniper the men catch.

While the South Africans go to look for the wounded German lieutenant, Heinrich, disarmed as he is, is suddenly surrounded by three scoundrelly Italians, "Partisans of the Thirteenth Hour," as they are called, for they were on the Fascist side as long as it was winning. They begin to kick and beat Heinrich, but are checked by a genuine Partisan, a middle-aged woman called Helena, and put to flight by the return of Meyer and Boshoff carrying the wounded German lieutenant. Helena disappears to fetch water and bandages for Heinrich's feet. Then a doctor and two medical orderlies appear to carry the lieutenant and Heinrich to the field hospital.

But they are interrupted by the appearance of Colonel Venter himself. He has heard that Liebenberg has been wounded by a sniper. When he finds him dead, he is overwhelmed with grief. This reaction quickly changes into deep-seated rage as he gives commands that Heinrich, who killed Liebenberg, and who, he insists, is a sniper, shall be shot. The others are horrified. The doctor refuses to allow it: the Germans are wounded prisoners and are therefore under his command, not Venter's. Venter points out that only the lieutenant is wounded; all that is wrong with Heinrich is that his feet have been lacerated with sores and stones and thorns. A passionate argument arises between the Jew, Meyer, and the Christian, Venter. Venter says the guilt for the murder of millions of Jews rests not upon a few leaders only but on every German who bears arms. Both men are eloquent with passion. Meyer points out that if they behave like Nazis all the blood of the war will have been spilt in vain. Venter remains obdurate. But not one of his men will shoot the prisoner. Venter then says he will shoot the man himself; and when Heinrich begs to be allowed to shoot himself instead, he denies him even that favor.

The two men go off stage, leaving the rest shuddering with expectation. A shot is heard; Venter comes back putting away his revolver, quite satisfied. At this moment, Helena reappears with a basin of water and some bandages. She and Venter look at each other. "Where is the boy?" she asks; and the curtain goes down as they are still gazing with the antagonism of two like and very strong characters into each other's eyes.

Though one part of the play which should be charged with violent feeling seems too coldly handled to be dramatic or poetic in that particular and important portion of the whole, poetic and dramatic qualities do inform, to a large extent, the entire play. The argument between Meyer and Venter, though the sort that people do have, is too like one in a Shaw play. It is interesting as an illustration of differences of opinion and temperament, but not, at that stage of the play, dark and deep and illogical enough: the words do not come from deep enough in the subconscious depths of men's minds, as they in reality do under pressure of the circumstances and as the passions presented to us by Uys Krige

would cause them to do. For example, there is no such "touch of
nature" as that in Uys Krige's own *Skietgebed van die Skollie*
(Hurried Prayer of the Colored Delinquent), in which the character, facing his judge and in the extremity of his terror, skips over
the "Prince Jesus" to whom he is praying; and seeing his own
mother sitting in the court with the tears stealing down her grey
cheeks, he addresses himself to God's mother, who, he instinc-
tively feels, will be softer-hearted than a just God: "O, help my,
mammie van die Lam, gou! gou!" ("Oh, help me, mammy of the
Lamb, quick! quick!") The word "mammie" shows feelingly what
is going on in his subconscious mind.

Despite the inadequacy at this point of *Die Sluipskutter* however, Uys Krige has not in any way shirked the grimness of Venter's character. Venter is very well drawn as a person of great
strength and of deep affections—a man who, having started his
life as a soldier during the Boer War, when, at the age of twelve,
he shot five Englishmen, has gained self-confidence and self-
sufficiency the hard way, by earning them. It is chiefly the depth
of his affection for his godson and for the boy's parents that rouses
the profound anger that overwhelms him at the boy's senseless
death; it is also his hatred of the tyranny which the Germans seem
to him to represent, and his loathing contempt for their snipers,
who, at the end of the war they have lost, continue to snipe when
nothing can save them: "Another sniper, eh?—filth that you are!
Lice, yes, lice . . . you creep into your holes where you're safe,
and then, when we can't see you and know nothing of you, you
shoot us in the back! And as soon as it gets a little too hot for you,
out you creep, you just stick up a white flag. Manly, isn't it? Very
manly! Hitler's heroes who fight to the death, to the last man—
only the last man to die is always ours!"

Uys Krige makes one realize strongly that he is past reason and
justice, and he does not in the least sweeten the bitterness of the
almost inevitable ending. The ending, in fact, comes, for all its
inevitability, with a shock, almost of surprise. Trusting the author's obvious good-nature, one has been saying: "The writer will
make some accident happen, or some persuasive argument." But
Uys Krige looks at the facts he has created with clear eyes: Venter
is not in the least a hard man. On the contrary, he faithfully and
well loves other men. Nor is he a narrow man. He hated what the
English did to South Africa in the Boer War; but, when the kaiser

began to bully small nations, he joined to help the English against him. In 1939 he again helped the English because he loathed with all his soul what Hitler was doing to Europe and to the Jews. But he is a strong man, one used to taking full responsibility for his own actions without self-doubt, no matter how much other people may blame him. He is convinced that Heinrich is a sniper; in these circumstances he detests and despises snipers; and, though he swears that as a soldier he always does what he does in cold blood, at the bottom of his decision there is not only cool determination but also its very opposite, passionate grief. Yet one feels that he takes both into account, accepts both as valid reasons for doing what he does; and he can therefore meet without wavering the accusing gaze of the equally strong and compassionate Helena. Her compassion is for the living man before her, the German; Venter's is for the dead whom he has loved.

The result of the writer's making the audience *feel* instead of merely *see* the feelings of the various characters at this point is that the spectator's suspense mounts and mounts as the action goes on. And as the scene gathers to its end, fear and hope alternate in him with painful agitation. He feels the shuddering suspense of Venter's subordinates as he goes off stage; and he waits for the shot as the men do with the horror that makes Meyer cover his ears and jerk back his head when it comes. The situation becomes absolutely real.

Also a war play, *All Paaie Gaan na Rome* is deeply and genuinely felt, and well managed. The main character, an old Italian women of between fifty and sixty who lives in the village of Castelmánica among the Abruzzi Mountains, is waiting along the roadside for a military truck in the hopes of getting a lift to Rome. With her is her little granddaughter of eleven, who is dumb, as the result, one discovers later, of a bomb attack on Rome in which her father was killed beside her. She has been staying in Castelmánica for the sake of the change. Now the grandmother has heard from a Major Ross that a doctor has newly arrived in Rome who can probably cure Gina if she comes soon.

In the course of the play five trucks are heard off stage, arriving, stopping; their drivers speak to the old woman and then pull away again. And her anxiety and that of the child and the suspense of the audience grow more and more intense as the darkness and the winter cold increase. The driver of the first truck is

very sympathetic, but he dare not overload his truck any further
or it will never make its proper journey; he recommends that the
old woman try the truck following his. But that one is not going to
Rome—its destination is Avezzano, which is useless to the old
woman. When the next truck arrives, she and the child are fore-
stalled by two pretty girls who appear at the last moment, jump
into the truck, which can take only two extra people, and are welcomed by soldiers who are not much concerned about having no
room for Gina and her grandmother. "It's only natural," sighs the
grandmother, "one is only young once." At this moment the noise
of another truck is heard, but this one takes no notice of the woman's signal and does not even stop; as it recedes, the sound of loud,
coarse, almost mocking laughter is heard. The noise of a fifth
truck is heard; this time the old woman is almost frantic; she
shows the driver the five stars on her bosom and tells him rapidly
about her five sons shot by the Germans for aiding escaped Allied
prisoners of war. They had hidden a group of exhausted men escaping from the Nazis after the fall of Mussolini in a cave. Her
husband and her five sons used to visit them with food and drink
and cigarettes. One day, as they were all sitting there chatting in
the winter sun outside the grotto, the Nazis surprised them un-
armed. Only the husband escaped. As he looked back from the
shelter of a hut he saw his five sons being put up against the rock
and machine-gunned to death.

The driver is moved; he himself, while escaping, had experienced the extraordinary courage and kindness of the Abruzzi Partisans. He climbs down, comes on to the stage, and listens, very
moved, while the old woman tells her story. But he cannot take
her to Rome. He promises, however, that in ten days' time, if she
hasn't got a lift before then, to take her and Gina to Rome. He
takes off his blouse and puts it round the shivering child; gives the
woman a blanket, a shirt, and some spare shoes and socks that he
has in the truck; and bids them both a heartfelt "totsiens" (till we
meet again). After praying to the Virgin in a shrine by the way-
side, the woman and child trudge off homewards, but they intend
to try for another truck ride on the morrow.

Simple as this story is, the play has a great deal of reality and is
at times very moving. It has indeed that undeniably real humanity
of which *Fuente Sagrada* falls short. The story acts itself out in
such a way that one feels acute anxiety growing as truck after

truck fails the grandmother and her charge—one is tensed for the outcome each time, and time after time one's eyes fill with tears. The silent, stoical child who begins to weep only after the third disappointment, and who tries so hard, even though she cannot control her shivering, to deny that she is cold; the patience, endurance, and tolerance of the grandmother; the kindness of the first, and the horror-stricken gratitude of the last truck-driver—all are drawn with a home-felt reality. So too is the grimness of the situation when the soldiers, with far from unselfish motives, load up the two young girls instead of the grandmother and Gina. Then, there is much in the texture of the play that is homely and real; for example, the grandmother attempts to comfort Gina—when after their penultimate disappointment they decide to go home but to try again next day—by describing the supper she will cook of hot tomato soup and macaroni with tomatoes and cheese. Most moving of all are such details as the picture called up so vividly in one's mind by the old woman's words of the Italians, the husband and the five sons, sitting sociably in the winter sun outside the cave chatting to the escapees just before their cruel fate overwhelms them: it suggests so powerfully the sweetness of life to them.

There is only one small touch in the play that strikes a false note—that of the grandmother's prayer to the Virgin, which seems to come a little self-consciously from the playwright rather than from the woman. Such a detail too as, "And if the doctor has to cut at Gina's throat, make his hand calm, *calm as thy gaze, Maria*" [my italics], and the too facile pacificism of "Give us love . . . so that it will never, never happen again." The unreality of hoping for a millenium is out of place in a play with so much reality in it.

As a result of Krige's experience in seeing the play produced, it has been improved (though again with some loss of naturalness in the dialogue) in the English version published in *The Dream and the Desert* and in the later Afrikaans version in G. J. Beukes' anthology of one-acters, *Woord en Masker* (Word and Mask). In the revised English play, two more soldiers come on to the stage, adding much to the liveliness and naturalness of the play; and the final prayer has been cut but not enough. In the improved Afrikaans version, the speeches originally written in English to indicate that they are not in Italian are now in Afrikaans; this removes a certain awkwardness by making the audience accept the story without being forced into the unnecessary realism of imagining some of the dialogue in a foreign language.

Alle Paaie Gaan na Rome is a play of great humanity and beauty; it well deserves the popularity and praise which it has received.

CHAPTER 6

The Full-Length Plays

I *Magdalena Retief*

ALL South Africans not in sympathy with the present government—and many who are—are so thoroughly sick of the exploitation, for political purposes, of "The Great Trek," as it is called, that it is hard for them to imagine enjoying any play or story about a theme so obsessively overemphasized and now so stale. Yet even they must enjoy Uys Krige's first published play, *Magdalena Retief*, which has this very theme. At the time when Uys Krige wrote it (1938) Afrikaner Nationalism still managed to be, for many of its adherents, comparatively free from Nazi and Fascist infection; and it was not until 1939, with the outbreak of World War II, that the poet openly declared himself to be in the opposite camp.

Magdalena Retief, in fact, was written for what turned out to be (though it was supposed in the beginning not to be) a great Nationalist occasion: the centenary celebrations of the Great Trek itself. These included a drama competition for plays on a relevant theme, and *Magdalena Retief* won the first prize of fifty pounds, was performed at Krugersdorp as part of the festivity, was played thereafter about thirty times, and on the whole proved a popular success. It has been through many impressions since and has been drastically revised; and the improved version, with one not very good scene left out and with an excellent new one substituted, was published in 1948 by Unie-Volkspers Beperk. Both editions are beautifully embellished, by the way, with woodcuts by the distinguished artist, Cecil Higgs.

In this play Uys Krige accepts the idea on which all Afrikaners were brought up: the root cause of the Great Trek was dissatisfaction with the way in which the citizens and the farmers (English settlers and Afrikaners both) on the border of the Cape Colony in and near Grahamstown were treated by the British government. The play tacitly rejects the concept of some recent historians that the borderers were naturally lawless men whose chief object was to escape from the rule of law. But to discuss a matter which now more than ever before in history since then provokes hot and violent emotions on both sides of the question is not the purpose here. In any case, there is no doubt that the trekkers were people of great courage and fortitude to venture as they did by oxwagon far into the unknown hinterland, into all the hardships of pioneering and the dangers of famine, wild animals, and hostile Africans.

The story of how Piet Retief and seventy of his men, including two of his sons, were massacred by the Zulu chief, Dingaan, at Umghunghunghlovo, forms the climax of the play. The outline of this episode is well known in South Africa: the trekkers under Retief wished to settle in the Province of Natal and made a contract with Dingaan, the Paramount Ruler. Dingaan invited them into his kraal to conclude the treaty, first asking them to leave their weapons outside, which they did; his men entertained them with dancing; then at a given signal the dancers snatched weapons buried under the floor, slaughtered their guests, and proceeded to the almost unprotected camps—to a place afterwards called "Weenen" or "Weeping" in memory of the event—and to others, where they murdered every man, woman, and child. These events were afterwards avenged at the Battle of Blood River, where the Zulu power was broken for many decades; but the Battle of Blood River does not form a part of *Magdalena Retief*, except for the hint that it will come.

Uys Krige, though extreme Nationalists now refuse, because he is not one of them, to accept him as "a true Afrikaner" is himself an indirect descendant of two of the bravest and most famous of the Voortrekker leaders, Pieter Retief on his father's side and Pieter Lafras Uys on his mother's. The city of Pietermaritzburg, capital of the Province of Natal, is named after these two Pieters and after a third brave leader, Gerrit Maritz.

Krige takes as his central figure Magdalena, the wife of Piet Retief. He was first fascinated by her character when he read in Gustav Preller's *Piet Retief* a letter written by her to her relatives in the Cape Colony in the year 1840, the first she had written for four years. She begins by saying: "things go well with me and my four children . . . beyond expectation, and still more beyond our deserts. . . . With regard to the enemy, we live in peace with him," she says;

he has paid us damages for cattle and loot. . . . But it is brave and has cost us dear that we voortrekkers had to begin from the beginning again, whereby I am so stripped of goods and blood—first robbed of husbands and children by the cruel enemy—and the measles robbed me of grandchildren and a brave son-in-law, my Debora's husband. . . . Dear brother, at your request I will tell you how many children I have had and how many I still have. By the late Jan Greyling I had nine children; three died small, six I reared—of them are dead my Gertruida in childbed, my second daughter, Maria, of the palpitations, both were married, and my son Jan was murdered by the Kafirs—he and his late father, Jan Greyling, had to leave their lives there inland and to give their bodies to the wild beast. And here my brave husband Retief and my youngest son Pieter Retief and my eldest son, Abraham Greyling, also had to give their bodies to the animals, through the cruel Dingaan. Dear brother, my disasters are almost too heavy for me to mention. Think, two husbands and three sons I had to yield up for whom I could make no grave. By Retief I also lost two children in infancy—by Greyling I still have alive Piet and Bêrend, and by Retief, Jacobus Francois. His wife and children are also dead; then I still have Magdalena Margareta—her children are also dead—now of my fifteen children I still have five. Dear brother send me a box of little trees—I will pay for the transport.

The play, consisting of eight scenes, is constructed rather awkwardly—which is not surprising in a first play. About a decade elapses between the first and the second scenes, another between the second and the third, and yet another between the third and the fourth. Only then does the action leading up to the climax, the news of the massacres and the imminence of a Zulu onslaught on the speakers, get thoroughly under way. A more experienced playwright would possibly have managed to get all the facts and the characterization that are contained in the first three scenes into one scene of exposition. Not that the play, even in the first three scenes, ever drags—everything in it, though the theme, the action, and the characterization are all simple, holds the attention both by its inherent interest and by the fact that there is something active going on on the stage all the time. The various women, the spirited children, even the baby in the cradle—all have at least a spark of individual character; and, as for the two chief personages, Pieter and Magdalena Retief, a sense of something great in each of them is slowly and very substantially built up.

By the end, one knows Piet Retief not only as a manly man, a man born to lead and to command, to feel for and help others, to triumph over catastrophe (like his bankruptcy in Grahamstown) and gain new strength from it, but a man also of a more capacious mind than most of his followers. For example, he never regards the Africans, including Dingaan, merely as "the enemy," but believes it possible to live in amity with them. And there is an element of real tragedy, of course, in the fact that this belief is so cruelly betrayed. As for Magdalena, her spirit rides one storm after another with a controlled strength like that in her letter. She is a compassionate soul: she and her husband both treat their slaves like valued members of the household. On going bankrupt, for example, they keep two of the slaves, for it would be a crime, they say, to sell old Mina and Robert of Mozambique, who have served them so long; and the younger slaves they sell to a cousin, so that they will still be in the family and well looked after.

Magdalena's last words in the play, foreshadowing Blood River and spoken after unendurable strain when help at last is at hand, are grim indeed: "Dingaan . . . false heart . . . now we shall see . . . now we shall see." But the epilogue shows her towards the end of her life as an old woman living alone, poor and forgotten, with her ancient servant Mina in a "hartebeeshuisie" [1] in the town of Pietermaritzburg, making a living for both of them by baking and selling "beskuit" [2] and knitting, and poor as she is, not pressing for payment from those who are poor themselves, but sturdily demanding it from those who are merely stingy. She does not repine: her spirit survives everything, like the naked willow trees outside her window. "How cold and bare," she says in the last words of the epilogue, "but how steadfast and strong those willow-trees are in the winter."

The play contains exciting action and a good deal of poetic feeling. Anyone who reads the seventh scene, for example, in which news arrives of the horror at Umghunghunghlovo and Weenen, and the approach of a Zulu attack upon the Retief lager,[3] cannot do so "without a tighter breathing and zero at the bone." [4] If well acted, this play must be even more exciting to see.

And there are signs throughout this simple play that Uys Krige is here also what he has proved himself to be in his verse writings: a natural poet. In many of the scenes the pervading mood is admirably evoked by all kinds of unobtrusive means—for example, the feeling of foreboding in the scene in which Debora has a nerve-storm of fear and misery at the mere thought of embarking on the Trek, or the lovely later scene at what was afterwards called Rooirosekrans, where an impression of the paradisical loveliness of the flowery slopes of the Drakensberg is made to emanate from everything that is said, but is dramatically changed as the light fades and Magdalena exclaims: "But what a fearful great shadow the mountain throws! Just now there were such long streaks of light here, and now the whole lager is black!"

The texture is richer than these translated quotations can show. But the play, as a whole, is too simple. It has genuine human and poetic feeling, and that rare quality, the ability to move reader or audience, yet perhaps the poet writes as yet with too little economy to make his effects as consistently strong as they should be.

II *Die Twee Lampe*

Twee Lampe (Two Lamps), Uys Krige's second full-length play, was first published in the Afrikaans version by Afrikaanse Pers Beperk in 1951. Early in 1964 Hollands-Afrikaanse Uitgewers Maatskappy (H.A.U.M.) published a translation and revision of it under the title of *The Two Lamps*. There are certain awkwardnesses in the dialogue of the English version, especially in the management of the respectful form of address to parents, older people, and authorities, like schoolmasters, where custom demands in the Afrikaans the use of the third instead of the second person, for example, "Father told me himself that Father wouldn't go."

This form is adopted in the English version, yet Ilse calls her mother "Mum," when "Marm" or "Marmmie" would be more in key. Also the archaic inflection in the prayer at the end is wrong: "thou chastiseth" and "hath thou" for "thou chastisest," "hast thou." And sometimes the proverbs and idioms sound strange: "And I didn't sell it for an apple and an egg" instead of "for an old song," or "The apple doesn't fall far from the tree" for "You're a chip of the old block." Perhaps the intention in this last matter is to make reader or audience realize that everybody is speaking Afrikaans, but it doesn't quite work. However, all these minor matters could be very easily adjusted before a performance or before the next printing of it.

[78]

Yet despite these faults, the English version is a great improvement of the original. In the Afrikaans version the suicide of Frans seems insufficiently prepared for, and so does Sybrand's suicide; but in the English, by means of many slight changes, both are made altogether more credible. This improvement is particularly true of the rearrangement in a couple of scenes. In the English version the reaction to Frans's suicide is not shown at all, nor is the suicide even quite clearly established until the scene three months later, which follows the one in which Frans goes off "like one possessed." This does away with the sudden shock of it and prepares the mind to accept it as more credible when it comes. In the case of Sybrand's suicide, a longish exchange between Cornelia and the father between Sybrand's rushing out of the room and the fatal shots being heard has the same kind of effect. The mind has more time to take in what is about to happen, and is therefore more able to believe it. There are many other improvements as well, and the whole English version is therefore so much better than the Afrikaans one that it should be discussed instead of the other.

The action takes place in the 1860's; old Gert Beukes, once poverty-stricken,[5] is now the owner of Buffelsfontein, the richest farm in the Swellendam district, a stern, bare country situated near the mouth of a great river that forms a maelström among the rocks not far from the house, and, passing a little fishing village, flows into the sea. In the course of the play he buys another farm, Kranskop. Gert Beukes, a forbidding and lonely person, is wedded to his religion and particularly to the savage, threatening parts of the Old Testament. He works himself as relentlessly as he works his Colored laborers; his two sons, Frans and Sybrand; and his niece-housekeeper, Cornelia. He has lost, by lingering illness, his two young daughters, Anna and Heleen, and the wife for whom he toiled for twelve long years to gain, but who never loved him. Now, because he hates poverty, believing that those who are as poor as he once was remain so only because they have no gumption, he lives only to increase his wealth and to improve his farms so that he may leave everything to his two sons, whom (though they can have no inkling of it because of his undemonstrative and harsh treatment of them) he loves.

The first scene opens with Frans making love on the river mouth bank, their trysting place, to Ilse Johannsen, a charming, affectionate, natural girl, whose father, Erik, a fisherman, is a man who cares nothing at all about money, religion, position, and convention and who is very often penniless and drunk. Frans wants to marry Ilse; asks consent of Erik and his wife Sannie, who gladly give it; and then goes home with a quaking heart to tell his father. Gert is beside himself with rage. Poverty and agnosticism are the two sins he can least forgive, and Erik is guilty of both, Gert, refusing to hear of the marriage, packs Frans off to look after the totally undeveloped Kranskop. A month later, somewhat softened, Gert goes to visit Ilse to ask her to give Frans up for at least a year. With Erik's encouragement, Ilse decides that it will be best, after all, for Frans if she accepts an offer to sail to Europe two days later on the ship *Skaggerak,* which is then lying in the harbor, to be governess for the eighteen months of the trip to a Norwegian family now on board. She does not tell Frans of her intention, but she writes a letter to be delivered to him after she has gone.

Meanwhile, Frans has been eating his heart and wearing his nerves out in what amounts to solitary confinement at Kranskop, which is utterly desolate and lonely. The place is always so fog-enshrouded that his state of mind becomes desperate, and the only thing that keeps him going is his visits to and the prospect of visits to Ilse. He is at Buffelsfontein when Sybrand, without any preparation, breaks the news that Ilse has sailed away on the *Skaggerak.* Distraught as Frans already is, this news is literally unbearable. He rushes out, leaps on to his horse, rides straight to the maelström, and flings himself into it. Later one learns that, because suicide is a deadly sin, Gert has deleted Frans's name from the family Bible.

Three months later, Gert comes into the room to find Cornelia and Sybrand talking intimately together. Immediately suspecting that they are in love, he attacks them brutally. Their protestations that they are only friends are coarsely contradicted. They are cousins, storms Gert; moreover, Cornelia is a penniless dependent, while Sybrand is heir to both Buffelsfontein and Kranskop; it is, therefore, unthinkable that he should marry a pauper like Cornelia—one fit only, he says crossly, to be a servant. Sybrand's angry protests only exacerbate the old man, and Sybrand in his turn is packed off to the solitary confinement and gloom of Kranskop.

Four months later, he comes back in a state of hopeless melancholy and tells Cornelia that he is determined to leave Kranskop and to come back to Buffelsfontein for good, come what may. Seized with religious doubts, he can no longer believe in the faith he was bred in nor that there is a life after death; and the idea that Frans is gone forever in such misery and that he will never see him again is unbearable to him. When his father comes in and Sybrand announces his intention, a terrible quarrel breaks out, in the course of which the son declares his loss of faith. This declaration makes Gert more implacable than ever, and finally Sybrand, dreadfully overwrought and seeing no joy or meaning or purpose in life, rushes out in despair. A shot is heard; Sybrand has killed himself. The old man, now utterly desolate with no purpose left in life now that he has no child to whom he can leave the two farms, nevertheless opens the great family Bible, draws a steady stroke through the name of his last remaining, and, strange as it may seem, beloved child, Sybrand. And as he does so, the curtain falls.

Uys Krige has worked at this play for fourteen years since he first wrote it in Afrikaans. The texture of the writing and the nuances of meaning in the actual words used that convey the total poetic effect remain better in the Afrikaans than in the English version, yet the many structural and other changes, and slight modifications make the English (as has been noted) a much better play than the Afrikaans. The English version has received a prize from America—one of the two Rosamund Gilder awards for plays from the continent of Africa translated into English, in a competition sponsored by the Maine Masque Theatre of the University of Maine, the Institute for Advanced Studies in the Theatre Arts, New York, and the United States National Commission for UNESCO. It still contains, however, a fault which the sober reflecting mind recognizes but which good acting and much emphasis on certain aspects of the story might disguise. The sober mind asks, "Why did no alternative to suicide present itself to either Frans or Sybrand?" (In the Afrikaans version, one is struck by the almost incredible fact that Frans does not even read the letter Ilse leaves for him; in the English version, this is not so conspicuous because of the gap of three months before we know that Frans has killed himself.) "Why didn't the two able-bodied young men leave home and find work for themselves?" is a question that should be answered somewhere in the play.

An answer is partly given in the mood created by a thousand

touches in the texture of the writing. The delicacy and sensitivity of Frans, his absolute dependence on Ilse for the love which alone can sustain his solitary life at Kranskop, the consuming melancholy into which the unwholesomeness and fog and gloom and terrifying loneliness of the hard, bare, empty farm plunge him— all these create a mood of depression and evil expectation in which the suicide of Frans seems natural enough. In Sybrand's case, the sense of the loneliness and gloom of Kranskop is intensified by many details; moreover, the playwright shows how deep misery has eaten into his heart when, to the senseless death of his beloved brother, are added the horror of his father's implacable character, the deprivation caused by Gert's prohibition of his friendship with Cornelia, and the cruel memory of the deaths of his mother and two young sisters. And when one discovers, in a conversation with Erik, how this melancholy is intolerably intensified by his inability to accept either his father's religion or Erik's sturdy and cheerful humanism, one finds Sybrand's suicide even more understandable than Frans's. If these things were emphasized in production, the play could not fail to move.

The central tragedy of the play comes through quite powerfully: the way in which old Gert Beukes destroys every chance of happiness for himself as well as for everybody else, and kills what he most loves by trying too hard to mold his two sons into his own barren strength. Certain passages that have escaped the attention of various critics should be made the most of by producers. They are: Cornelia's frequent assertions that Gert does what he does out of love for his sons; Gert's conversation with Erik's wife, Sannie, when he confides in her, because he likes and trusts her, that after he had waited fourteen years to marry the woman he loved, his children were conceived in coldness of heart. Consequently one feels that his sexual life has been frustrated and that he is pitiably jealous of both Frans and Sybrand, who are ardently loved, though in Cornelia's case the love is friendship as yet.

Also there is Gert's much softened manner in his discussion with Ilse; and, when he begs her to leave Frans free for a while and when he argues that the twenty-year-old Frans is too young for marriage, these words carry weight. There is Cornelia's account of how she found the old man secretly weeping all night in the utmost bitterness of grief over Frans's bier. There are Cornelia's gentle arguments to Gert after Sybrand has rushed out of the house: she actually succeeds in persuading him that he should talk sympathetically to Sybrand; but her success comes too late, for the next moment the fatal shot explodes on their ears.

Finally, there is Gert Beukes' heartbroken last soliloquy, just before he sits down at the table with awful ceremony, pulls the great Bible to him, and deletes Sybrand's name. This soliloquy consists mainly of passages from the Book of Job, for, unhappily for Gert, after a few moments of insight into his own guilt, he sees himself as Job, though the words themselves are heavy and dreadful with grief. All these things emphasize the painful conflict and its most bitter ending, which is the main theme of the play: the conflict between Gert's unexpressed love of his sons, the two lamps of his life; and his unadaptable principles of education, which extinguish both lamps and leave him in the darkness of utter desolation. He is typical of South Africa, of its "granite" Calvinist rulers, capable of feeling, who destroy life by their rigidity and self-righteousness.

A great quality in this play is the way the whole is permeated with a strong sense of the landscape of the setting: the character of that austere beauty of sand dunes and river mouth, mist and sea, is felt with as much reality as the character of any of the dramatis personae. Erik Johannsen's gay, amusing descriptions of his catches of fish—their multitude and glitter and color and liveliness; the sound of the *Skaggerak*'s siren breaking into the dialogue every now and then, at first suggesting the romance of faraway lands and of seafaring but later sounding alarming and ominous; the cry of the kiewiet from time to time; the mewing of sea-birds; later, the sense of mist shrouding and choking everything; the music that floats across the river from a party on the opposite bank; the sad strain that steals into the house towards the end as Apools, the Colored man, plays on his concertina—all of these produce a strong sense of place, of the life of the place weaving into the lives of the characters, or going on heedlessly despite them. At the same time these touches throw a sort of poetic aura round the action which enlarges and beautifies it. Poetry is Uys Krige's right hand and prose is only his left; and it is interesting that, as his qualities ripen and fill out more and more, his plays become more poetic. As "theater," too, if that much misused word means stage success, *The Two Lamps* is apparently extremely effective. Audiences are much moved by it, weep at its denouément, and write letters to the author, begging him to be merciful to old Gert. And this reaction is certainly evidence of its ability (without which no work of art can succeed) to communicate emotion.

III *Die Ryk Weduwee*

Uys Krige's third full-length play, *Die Ryk Weduwee* (The Rich Widow) is a comedy. The comedy resides chiefly in the characters and texture of the play, for the plot is simple. Anna de Kock at forty-four, having lost her loving and beloved husband, has been a handsome widow for two years. She has one son, now twenty-four, who is a composer of some fame and a university lecturer in music. Anna has inherited, inter alia, a beautiful fruit farm in the Wellington district (Western Cape Province), which flourishes under the management of Piet Swart, much the same age as she. The house is managed just as capably for her by a youngish housekeeper, called Bettie Roos.

At "Soete Inval," as the name indicates,[6] there is open house; and, on the glorious day on which the play opens, people pour into the house, all, it appears, bent on one purpose—to persuade Anna to marry again. First there is her old friend, Christine Vermaak, show-prize-winner and queen of canned-fruit making and of all household arts; then her son Jan arrives on a two weeks' vacation and attempts the same persuasion, from which even Bettie does not stand aloof. Next, what seems like a stream of suitors arrives: first, Professor Etienne Roux, an eccentric elderly bachelor who is Professor of Literature at the University of Natal; second, one Frans de Waal, a dignified widower of sixty, who has never seen Anna before but who likes her and proposes within the first ten minutes; and third comes the widower, Pierre de la Motte Naude, a lawyer and also a farmer, who still mourns the death and sings the praises of his wife Debora, deceased slightly more than a year before. He is so bent on marrying the unknown rich widow that, taking Bettie for the owner of "Soete Inval," he proposes to her; next, seeing Christine, he proposes to her. Fortunately both women soon undeceive him; and, when he finally meets Anna, he is still a free man and can make a third attempt, quite undeterred, to gain a wealthy bride. All these guests are received by Anna (and even by one another) with the greatest good-humor; and, though she does not intend to accept any of her suitors and rebuffs all her advisers, Anna cordially invites them all to stay to lunch. Thus ends the first act.

In the second act, a couple of days later, Jan has just told his mother that he will cease to be able to compose if he doesn't break away from lecturing and get to Europe for a year. She had just offered to finance his trip when de Waal calls again, this time accompanied by his young daughter, Alida. Jan and Alida fall deeply in love at first sight, and Jan abandons all idea of going to Europe on the spot—until he hears that Alida too has been promised a year there by her father. Next, Roux and Naude, in comradely spirit, work each other up to the sticking point of proposing to Anna, and both are rejected. A black southeaster comes up, and all marriage plans are companionably shelved when the foreman summons the guests to help pick the guavas quickly before they are blown down and the crop ruined; finally, when the guests have all gone, Anna receives a letter which makes her turn pale and pass it onto her son. It appears that she is ruined—her brother-in-law has lost all her money as well as his own through speculation; and, instead of paying off the bond on the farm with the money she has been sending him every month, he has lost that too. Jan springs into the breech: they will have to sell the farm, and then they'll get a little house in Cape Town. Europe and marriage can wait; he will support his mother easily on his salary and by giving concert tours during vacations.

Act III is unexpected. Every one of Anna's suitors, especially Naude, had in proposing to her had at least one eye on her property. But, now that she has lost everything, every one of them comes back, even the self-same or the very next day with offers of help and with renewed proposals of marriage. Christine, too, arrives with huge bunches of flowers and with doughty arguments in favor of her cousin, Etienne Roux. But Anna insists that she has no need of help and no wish to marry. Finally the manager, Piet Swart, hears of Anna's plight; reveals that he has been in love with her since they were both at school in Stellenbosch, that he has three rich farms of his own, that he has taken the job as manager only to be near her; and begs her to marry him. He, too, is refused, but more reluctantly. Then, while everybody is still in the house, Jan comes running into the room: his uncle has telephoned: things are not nearly so bad as he thought—the farm need not be sold; the money can in time be recovered. And the play ends with Jan playing the piano, while everybody dances for joy right in the middle of the stage. Anna dances with Piet Swart (whom she has specially sent for).

There is no fault to find with *Die Ryk Weduwee*. It is so delightful that one is not surprised that it had a long run with National Theatres Organisation or that it made about twenty-four thousand pounds. The play is extremely amusing to read, and must be very much more so to watch: it overflows with comedy of every kind: laughable situations, laughable characters, laughable actions. Properly produced, it should raise gale upon gale of laughter from the audience; and the report is that it does. The mere actions of the characters on the stage are divertingly ludicrous. For example, Etienne Roux, who is a fanatic about fresh air, silent contemplation, and physical exercise, is apt at odd moments to be seen through the window walking about on the stoep on his hands. He inspires his new and elderly friend, the paunchy and very unathletic Naude, to imitate some of his feats, which Naude in his innocence does with ridiculous effect, and so on.

Then, too, the characters are remarkably funny. Etienne Roux, for example, is a mine of happy absurdities, and it is characteristic of him that, the first time he means to propose, he is talking so enthusiastically about all kinds of other things that he doesn't manage to fit the proposal in—as he says apologetically afterwards: "I forgot." The most absurd character of all is the nevertheless not unlikeable Pierre de la Motte Naude, who precedes every one of his wrongly aimed proposals with a breathless account of his property, his ancient name, and the posts of honor he holds in the church and in the community, pads out his eloquence every few moments with stately quotations from the Bible, yet rather takes the edge off his declarations of devotion by constantly quoting his dear, departed Debora, whose price was above rubies, the model of all the female virtues. Poor Naude is converted from his avarice by the generous hospitality and goodheartedness of "Soete Inval," but he is so lost without a wife and so anxious to marry again that, when Anna refuses him for the second time, he immediately approaches, first, Christine (not unregardful of her property), and finally the portionless Bettie once again in speeches of such passionate desperation that, like the good-natured Bettie, one almost longs to comfort him.

Intermingled with all these absurdities, there is a good deal of a different kind of comedy—the kind that contains self-criticism and high, gay intelligence: the exchanges between Jan and Alida, which, though amusing, are also rather moving in the mutual rapture of the lovers which shines through the lightness and gaiety of their words. Even the exchanges between them and Anna and Christine, for they too are quite clever, cultivated people, contain a good-humored play of wit and high spirits dance through most of their talk.

What particularly endears one to this play is the warm, generous life, the love of nature and country and people that informs it. The golden sunlight of the Boland (the Cape Western Province) pours through it: the beauty of the countryside and of the farm— its poplar groves, its pines, its citron and guava orchards, its wild flowers, its river and its gloriously sunny freshness—comes blowing in at the windows, as it were; and one is delightedly conscious of it all the time. The characters, despite the ludicrous failings of some of them, are all good-natured, friendly, and without malice; these qualities contribute to the sunny, magnanimous tone of the play. Above all, the comedy abounds in vitality: every one of the characters—the young lovers, Christine, Etienne, Bettie, even the comical and at first self-seeking Naude, and (in a different way, in the contained strength which one feels in them) Anna and Piet Swart—is brimming over with his own particular kind of vital liveliness, and the play sparkles and vibrates with it.

Add to this quality the music that ripples through it, classical music from under the skilled fingers of Jan de Kock, popular songs and dances from the clumsy ones of Naude (who thinks that, if trained, he could have outplayed Jan) and one has in this comedy a poetic whole that has amply earned the clamorous stage popularity with which it has been received. Even without the music it must win also the enthusiasm of the slow and savoring reader and rereader who sits thoughtfully at home in his own armchair.

IV   *Die Goue Kring*

Die Goue Kring, 'n Legende in Vier Bedrywe (The Golden Circle, a Legend in Four Acts), published in 1956 by Balkema of Cape Town and Amsterdam, is the last of Uys Krige's plays to have been thus far actually printed. There are others, like *Die Loodswaaiers* (The Leadswingers), ready for the press; there are also *Twaalfde Nag* (Twelfth Night) and *Yerma,* but these are translations, the first from Shakespeare and the second from Lorca; and none of these will be discussed in detail in this book. *Die Goue Kring* has been produced by amateurs with considerable success, but it has not yet been professionally done. It is, in fact, in the 1956 edition, a good deal too long for the stage; but the author is at present engaged in drastically cutting the play. This cut version is in every way, I think, an improvement upon the version of 1956—which, by the way is delightfully ornamented with drawings, very delicate and economical, by his artist brother, François.

Die Goue Kring is not tightly constructed, like *Die Ryk Weduwee,* with everything in the action strictly dependent on the main theme: it wanders a little waywardly and is, therefore, very difficult to summarize. The story happens in Spain, a country which has always charmed Uys Krige; it is based on an old Portuguese legend, or several legends. It is, therefore, a folklorish mixture of comedy, romance, and pathos.

The central figure is Moeder Mart (Mother Martha), an elderly peasant woman who makes a living near the village of Candamar by weaving lobster baskets for the fishermen and also by selling the oranges that ripen so plentifully in her little orchard. With her lives an orphan girl of eleven, whose name, Soledad (Spanish for "solitude"), exactly suits the strange, charming presence she always creates in this story as she goes silently about her occupations, serenely absorbed in whatever she happens to be doing.

When the play opens, Mother Mart's house is empty, for she and Soledad have gone to the market to sell her wares; and the first scene places one, as it were, in the orange grove, with, in one corner of the background, her cottage, of which the wall facing the audience, is "missing." Luis, a blind guitarist and poet, comes in search of Mother Mart; finding her away, he sits down on the bench under a big orange tree while he waits and composes and sings to himself a song in praise of that golden globe, or circle, the orange. The song ends with lines which may be roughly translated (leaving out all the music of words which in the Afrikaans fall very sweetly on the ear): "What shall we do with you, Orange?" and the eager answer comes: "I want to be a golden gleam through green/And then be picked, so reconciled with fate,/To be an orange only orange, orange, orange!"

While Luis is sitting happily singing to himself on a bench, the heads of two little boys, Pedro and Juan, pop up over a ruined wall—they are reconnoitering the terrain with a view to stealing a couple of pillowcases full of oranges while Mother Mart is at the market. But, Luis being aware of them, they drop their plan hastily and distract his attention with amusing chatter about births and deaths in the village since Luis was last there.

When the boys leave, Luis, left alone singing lightly his "Song of the Orange," becomes aware of a Stranger, a large, handsome young man, who congratulates him on a song that shows he neither fears death nor hoards for the moth and the rust. The Stranger's approach, however, makes Luis suddenly shiver. An odd conversation follows, interspersed with song; the Stranger teases Luis to guess who he is and why his presence so disturbs him; then, having found that Mother Mart is absent, he departs.

Pablo now appears, a stout, very lively, middle-aged fisherman with a wooden leg. He is in a state of intense irritation, and in wonderful torrents of eloquence he describes the shrewishness of his wife, Violetta: his health is poor, he is dreadfully tortured with rheumatism; he has, moreover, a wooden leg, his natural one having been heroically sacrificed at the Battle of Lepanto—in fact, his health is destroyed, yet his wife Violetta ("Of all names!" cries he) expects him to go out fishing for their living in unmerciful weather. At this point, Violetta bursts in, scolding, and despatches her now faltering husband on some household task, upon which Luis mockingly strums a snatch of his "Song of the Orange."

Next Isabella and Ferdinand present themselves. Isabella is the beautiful young daughter of Pablo and Violetta; Ferdinand, the handsome son of the widower, Miguel, who is not only the richest man in the district but is also obsessed with the need to pick up and hoard every bit of iron that he spies lying around—nails, screws, hinges (he has barns full of them). The two young people are head over heels in love, but Miguel objects. Luis makes a gay song in honor of the lovers, "The Song of the Betrothed Pair," and everybody, including Martha and Soledad, now back from the market, dances for joy; but Soledad is soon absorbed in a dreamy, graceful, solitary dance of her own. When the Stranger comes back and seems sorrowfully enchanted by Soledad's movements, one begins to suspect that he is Death; and one is reminded of Ben Jonson's words about the child, Salthiel Pavy, for whose death, he says, "Death's self is sorry."

The next act opens with Pablo, riotously expansive, "making a bravura entrance" by dancing towards Mother Mart's house on his wooden leg, juggling four mosbolletjies⁷ as he goes and singing a song about them as his four white doves. On his back is a knap-sack with a baking of these buns in it that he is bringing as a present from his daughter to the old woman. The mosbolletjies are presented; Ferdinand and Isabella announce their plan to marry in spite of Miguel; Pablo dilates with voluble expressive-ness on the evils of marriage; Violetta breaks in; an energetic and most eloquent dispute follows; Miguel is seen approaching; and Violetta and Isabella urge Pablo to put his gift of eloquence to good use by persuading Miguel to consent to the marriage.

As Miguel approaches, his eyes are fixed on the ground. Every now and again he bends to pick up a nail or a hinge, which he industriously polishes while making up and quietly singing a lov-ing little ditty in praise of it and which he then stows away in his pocket. Without waiting for Pablo, Violetta accosts him to de-mand his consent to the marriage. Her approach is received very gallantly, but Miguel tells her that his son is to marry Rosa, the daughter of rich Don Antonio. "Squint-eyed Rosa with the bandy legs?" interjects Viletta indignantly, and she then surprises one by a most ardent defence of her noble, heroic, badly-disabled hus-band, whom as the cleverest man in Candamar, Miguel should be proud to be allied to. He thinks so much, she says, that it is aston-ishing his head doesn't burst into a thousand pieces from trying to contain all the thinking that goes on at such a tremendous pres-sure inside it. Miguel freely admits all this. But—Ferdinand is poor! The others go off disgusted, and Miguel is left alone on the stage with Luis, who offers to make him a song about the nails he is always picking up. It is called "The Song of the Nail." I roughly translate the refrain of it, omitting, of course, and not imitating the clinking, hammering rhythm:

> Bring the coffin! Bring the hammer!
> I am fair, I am shining!
> Beat me in! Beat me in!
> I want to clink! I want to clink!

And the last refrain goes,

> I want to clink! I want to clink,
> Like an axe on the block!
> Beat me in! Beat me in!
> Tock! Tock! Tock! Tock!

Luis loudly plucks four chords on his guitar. Outraged, Miguel is telling Luis that his music has deteriorated when Marta appears at her front door. It is she whom Miguel has come to visit, with a request that he has made to her many times throughout the years: to marry her. His request is passionately sincere; and, when she refuses on the ground of his parsimony, he promises never again in all his life to pick up a nail, and he swears on his wedding-day to raise the wages of all the fishermen who work for him by one cent a day. She, in reply, urges his consent to the marriage of Ferdinand and Isabella; but over this proposal they clash. Miguel, left alone, upset, and miserable, presently spies a little hinge on the ground; and, polishing and singing lovingly to it, he begins to cheer up. At this, Luis, grinning, strikes up a funereal chord from "The Song of the Nail," and the rich man, starting angrily, stamps off the stage.

Luis has just begun the sparkling "Song of the Betrothed Pair," when the Stranger re-enters and suddenly shrill discords seem to be torn from his guitar. "You knew I was here," says the Stranger; "and you know who I am." Luis admits it; but, having accepted blindness, he feels he can accept death. However, he guesses that it is for Mother Mart that the Stranger has come. "I don't say so," says the Stranger.

But Mother Mart is out, and the Stranger decides to wait for her on the bench under the orange tree, while Luis departs to play at a town fiesta. Presently, while the Stranger is enjoying the delightful air and fragrance of the orange grove, Soledad and Mother Mart appear in the cottage—Mother Mart in the doorway of the off-stage kitchen; Soledad, in the living room. The Stranger's purposeful march to the cottage is arrested by the vision of Soledad on the threshold. Playing with oranges, she moves in a sort of slowly rocking dance as if to music, while she throws up the oranges and catches them again. He watches her, entranced; and, as she silently and gracefully dances off the stage, entirely absorbed, he follows her in a vain attempt to attract her attention. Meanwhile, Mother Mart has disappeared on business again.

Then our old friends, the two little boys, Pedro and Juan, reappear with pillowcases half-full of the oranges they have stolen from the rest of the orchard, and begin feverishly stripping the orange tree under which Luis and the Stranger have been sitting. The Stranger's sudden return stops them, and again they resort to talking hard to distract attention. Marta, coming back to find the stage empty and her orchard stripped, resolves to set a trap.

Act III, Scene I, shows the little square in front of the church of Our Dear Lady of the Sea in Candamar next morning. A beggar stands against the wall. First a bishop, then Ferdinand and Isabella, then Miguel, then Pablo and the two little boys pass by but ignore his plea for alms. The bishop acts as he does because he disapproves of beggars and so gives him a homily instead; Ferdinand and Isabella, because, though agreeing that true love extends itself to all the needy in the world, they are too absorbed in each other to hear him; Miguel, because he has just picked up a hinge and is delightedly singing a love-song to it; and Pablo and the boys, because they are all too fascinated by the story Pablo is telling of how he rescued his friend Andres from a boiling sea of eels.

But, when Marta and Soledad enter on their way to market with baskets of oranges, they give the beggar a couple of cents and a quantity of oranges, upon which he asks what he can do in return. Marta racks her brains and, choosing something impossible, says she would like anybody who touches a tree in her orchard to stick fast to it. To carry on the joke, she adds that she wouldn't like them to stick to it forever—perhaps it would be as well, if at a touch of her hand on his shoulder, the thief could be free. In departing, another thought strikes her: she says, no, at the first touch of my hand let him be given a little freedom of movement in a circle round the tree—let him be freed altogether only at a second tap on the shoulder. The beggar says it shall be so; and, as Marta goes off with Soledad, she remarks on his attractive appearance and pleasant manner.

Act III, Scene II, in a very lively manner shows Pedro and Juan trying once again to rob Marta's orange grove. To their absolute consternation they stick to the tree; Marta descends on them in righteous indignation; but, as she touches Juan twice on the shoulder by mistake, he is free and darts out of sight in a second. (He has the more sensitive and imaginative conscience of the two, in any case.) So Pedro alone still sticks to the tree, and Marta takes the opportunity of giving him a good hiding, through which he howls as dramatically as possible. At last she stops, and with one tap releases him from the tree trunk, though not from the invisible tether that prevents his getting away. Finally the kind, motherly woman gives him a second tap; and conducting him, limping energetically into the house for a glass of orange juice, she lets him go.

In Act III, Scene III, which takes place later in the same afternoon and is much more consistently serious than any other part of the play, Death at length finds Marta at home, tells her who he is and that he has come to take her away. Loving life despite many sorrows and not wishing to go, Marta hits upon the idea of sending him into the grove to pick her some oranges so that she can make them each a stirrup-cup of the juice before she sets off on the long, dusty journey with Death. Of course, Death sticks to the tree and calls out in rage for an axe; but Marta and Pablo, who happens to turn up, are delighted to see Death caught "like a wolf in a trap." As Pablo taunts the Stranger, the stage grows pitch dark, thunder rolls, lightning flashes; and the Stranger, now seen for what he is, the Skeleton Death, has the terrified Pablo in his arms. In these straits Pablo confesses that all his deeds of heroism, at Lepanto and in the boiling sea of eels, were imaginary; nevertheless, he has courage enough to feel that, in the midst of his terror at those dangers, he was more intensely alive than at any other time of his existence. Ferdinand rushes in to save Pablo, Isabella rushes in to save Ferdinand; there is another thunderclap; and, when the light returns, the Stranger is found in his pleasant shape again, nonchalantly standing with both hands fastened to the tree.

All the characters in the play now appear; and, though Death calls down thunder and lightning on them, he remains a prisoner. He calls for "The Dance of Death," but all the assembled characters, and others who run on to the stage, join in a "Dance of Life" instead, singing and dancing in praise of life and all its joys. Marta has just enough pity on him, however, to touch him once on the shoulder, so that he is able to walk round the tree as far as the invisible tether permits.

Act IV deals with the situation that has followed when Death has for some time been captive and unable to go about his usual work. At first everything has seemed wonderful: crops flourished, everything lasted, nobody died. But at length Marta is dreadfully disturbed to find that some old people, who have been longing in agony for life to end, find their suffering prolonged; and the climax is reached when she discovers that several women who were near their hour when the Stranger touched the tree cannot actually give birth and that the pangs of parturition are apparently to be prolonged forever. She therefore goes to the tree, much as she loves her life and loathes to give it up, and releases Death by another tap on the shoulder. And the play closes with Marta in her decent black shawl walking off into the distance beside the Stranger while Luis and Soledad, having sadly watched her go, quietly sing the "Song of the Orange" to the notes that Luis plucks gently on his guitar.

This long summary should give some inkling of how the ideas are managed in *Die Goue Kring*, but there is an itensity of life in the whole play, felt through every one of the characters, which it can hardly communicate. This presence is least obvious in the two silent ones, Soledad and Luis, where the life is gentle, but the strong sparkle of it in both is clearly seen. Mother Mart, who is calm, nevertheless moves through the action with considerable though controlled vigor and vital common sense. Love of life is more obvious in Isabella and Ferdinand, who talk not only of love but pack their dialogue with fun and youthful theorizing and argumentation. The mischievous adventurousness of the two little boys, Pedro and Juan, is also intense—to them the playwright has given the gifts of mimicry, mockery, and vivid language, which yet retain their childishness: they satirize what they observe with truly little-boy penetration. Their high spirits infect the reader— for example, when they chatter to Luis about the house they have built for themselves high up in an old oak tree, a house that even has a "kleinhuisie" (a little house, or lavatory); or when, showing a strong vein of comedy, they describe and imitate with poetic and creative zest, for Luis' benefit, the various ways in which the newborn babies of the village cry.

Then, the zest of both Violetta, the shrew, and Pablo, the loafer, is enormous. Whatever Violetta does is thoroughly done with all the vigor of a strong nature, whether it is keeping her house clean, giving her daughter moral support in her love affair, stoutly demanding Miguel's consent to the marriage, or (most often) scolding Pablo. In scolding him, she is trying by the sheer energy and industry of her abuse of him to drive him into showing some of these same qualities in the business of getting a living for the family. Her rhetoric at such times most vividly points her arguments and paints her disgust. Like all really vital people, she is unpredictable: one witnesses her spate of eloquence to Miguel in defence of the husband she is forever attacking (Pablo as he listens is as surprised as the audience, but he takes it all as earned, striking attitudes appropriate to the praise she showers on him).

In a way she is speaking the truth, for it isn't quite that Pablo lacks energy and industry; in imaginative oral composition, he has both. He is always embroidering his life with the richest arabesques of fantasy. When he pretends that the mosbolletjies he is juggling with are doves, for example, he addresses them so admiringly and so affectionately that one can imagine the white flesh of the buns turning into the feathers of soft white doves; one can also fancy, as the snowy objects fly up into the air and then down again, that they are really birds obedient to his command. Intense, too, are the sheer vigor of his inventive powers—the fancy and daring of his language and imagery, as when he tells, to an enchanted audience, of the terrible dangers he braved at "the greatest naval battle of all time," the Battle of Lepanto, or the horrors he defied when "without a moment's hesitation" he plunged into the fearful black slime and confusion of the sea of eels into which his friend Andrés had fallen, and gallantly pulled him out. When in the clutches of the skeleton Death, Pablo confesses that these stories are not true, and that, on the contrary, he behaved like a coward at Lepanto and towards Andrés, the vividness with which he describes his terror is instinct with the same intensity.

Even Miguel, the miser (who, by the way, is by no means caricatured or a mere figure of melodrama) has this zest. He is quite a pleasant fellow, ready to understand points of view different from his own; and the life-force beats in him a strongly as in any of the other characters. True, it expresses itself mainly in his enthusiasm for nails, screws, and hinges; but, in its own narrow way, it is quite a powerful force.

But the finest effect of *Die Goue Kring* with all its variety and drama is that it achieves a poetic whole of remarkable delicacy, vigor, and charm. Beaming from the center and setting of the play is Mother Mart's orchard; and, through all the characters and scenes of it, shines the symbol of the orange, that fruit which is round as the globe itself, golden as the sun that warms it, and which grows plentifully as anything in nature and has flesh that satisfies hunger and juice that quenches thirst. The orange is a golden round, circle, or globe; and the play is about how life, with its golden glory and its ever-renewed energy fresh as the sap of the fruit, must nevertheless be rounded off by death—it must, in fact, be consumed as the orange is eaten. For life without death would be a hideous thing.

The two characters who most sustain the poetic tone of the play are Luis, the blind guitarist, and the child Soledad. Luis observes, discerns, and compassionates—mostly in silence, or in playing his guitar, and in humming or singing one of the many ballads that echo and re-echo lightly through the action of the play: the happy "Song of the Orange," loveliest of all the ballads; the sparkling "Song of the Betrothed Pair"; the mocking "Song of the Nail," warning Miguel and all others of death; and all the little rhyming ditties, mere fragments, that the miser sings so besottedly to the tiny bits of "valuable iron" that he picks up and hoards in his great barns. These poems in their own right have in their style and extreme simplicity of language, rhythm, and rhyme the air of spontaneous composition by a minstrel for and among simple country folk. The effect of all this spontaneous music must be delightful when the play is properly produced on the stage—even the reader is conscious of the whole composition loosely caught up, as it were, in a net of music—an effect one sometimes notices in a wood when birds are singing.

As for Soledad, in her Uys Krige has managed by the actions and movements he "ascribes" to her in the stage directions (for she hardly speaks a single word) to create a presence that is felt whenever she appears and even after she has left the stage; it is almost as if she were a happy vision or a delighted and delightful spirit. Like Spenser's Una, who "made a sunshine in that shady place," Soledad seems to have a radiance of being that spreads around her and sets her apart in contented solitude from everybody else—within herself and with what she is doing at the moment she finds her joys, her complete absorption in merely being alive. She seems, however, not only a vision, but a real child; and one is reminded again of lines from Ben Jonson:

> Twas a child that so did thrive
> In grace and feature,
> As heaven and nature seemed to strive
> Which owned the creature.

That Soledad is a symbol of the simple force of pleasure in life —like what one feels on a sparkling day when the mere sunlight on the skin and the green leaves of a tree seem enchanting—is made explicit by the stanzas devoted to her in the song which all the characters sing as they dance round the captive Death. One verse of her song in the Afrikaans with its ecstatic, dancing, trembling rhythm follows:

> Sy dans, sy dans!
> Kyk net hoe bewe
> In haar die ritme
> Van die lewe.

A rough, literal translation of this would read:

> She is dancing, she is dancing!
> Look but how trembles
> In her, the rhythm
> of life.

Neither Luis nor Soledad plays much part in the plot of *Die Goue Kring;* but, as partly in *The Two Lamps,* and wholly in *Die Ryk Weduwee,* it is a sign of how far Uys Krige has travelled towards making plays that are also a poetic whole or a sort of dramatic poem (as most good plays used once to be, and perhaps should always be) that the evocation of tone, atmosphere and symbol is in this comedy-drama almost as indispensable a part of the total meaning as the action itself.

A play that mirrors such a variety of intense life cannot fail to be interesting. *Die Goue Kring* (of which the last act still needs cutting) is not so faultless as *Die Ryk Weduwee,* but it is more venturesome and of an unusual kind and quality. It confirms the impression that, though gifted with a strong dramatic sense, Uys Krige is never wholly himself except when he can escape the limitations of prose. As a dramatist, he began to create a new freedom for himself in *Die Twee Lampe*. He uses poetic freedom rather more fully in *Die Ryk Weduwee*, and in *Die Goue Kring* more fully still. And though *Alle Paaie Gaan Na Rome*, for example, is in some ways more successful than *Die Twee Lampe*, his new poetic freedom gives him a reach and range beyond that of his purely prose plays. And it makes the achievement of his last three published plays, in the chronological order in which they have been cited, stand above that of anything he has done in drama before them.

CHAPTER 7

The Poems

I Kentering and Rooidag

UYS KRIGE's first volume of poems, Kentering (Turning-point), appeared in 1935 when he was twenty-five years old; his second, Rooidag (Dawn, literally Red Day) in 1940. Most of the poems from both volumes, together with a few hitherto scattered juvenilia, appear in revised form in his Gedigte 1927–1940 (Poems) published in 1961 by van Schaik.

The poems in Kentering are mostly very slight, whether gay or melancholy, pithy or diffuse. The least successful are the most ambitious: those which touch upon the vastness and incomprehensibility of life with a youthfully solemn, ostentatious, unpenetrating melancholy—or those which give a false and unfelt moralizing or philosophizing twist to something otherwise true and felt. But nearly every poem in the book, however slight, bears one or more of the four marks by which the born poet may be recognized—either that genuine observation, which "the eye" unselfishly and unselfconsciously "on the object" [1] is capable of; or that spontaneous warmth of feeling that is growing so rare among writers; or a deep interest in the living language with an ability to use it with freshness, complexity, and force; or the gift of using rhythm to express meaning. Uys Krige's even then strong gift for rhythm builds up a poem like the excellent "Weerstand" (Resistance), for example, in which he praises the palm, the olive tree, and the deep-river-like stillness of a starry night as symbols of patience and resistance in words, sounds, and movements of mind that make the reader feel their being and personality, as it were, and realize with some vividness the nature of the qualities they symbolize. Poems like "Skans" (Bulwark), "Kontras" (Contrast), and "Nagreen" (Night Rain), short and simple as they are, are alive in the freshness and originality of their language; and minute cameos like "C.E. 93" (a description of a railway ganger's house alone on the empty veld seen from a passing train) and "Reisindruk"

(Impressions of Travel), unambitious as they are, have the same note of genuineness, the same touch of expressiveness in language and rhythm.

The best qualities of *Kentering* are nearly everywhere present also in *Rooidag* which shows, on the whole, a decided advance in experience. New attitudes appear—a more adult (but still youthful) kind of disillusionment; a strong sense of the comic; an aptitude for using anticlimactic, deflating rhymes with ironic effect. These are various signs of the influence of Continental thought and poetry of the 1930's—and, indeed, many of the poems were written in Europe. "Treursang vir van der Merwe" (Lament for van der Merwe), "Ballade vir Monsieur Lapeyre," "Barcarolle," and "Romanza" are examples of this progress. "Romanza" has a touch of the unfelt in its attempted tragedy; "Treursang vir van der Merwe" is the most complete and successful, the most felt, and also the most humorous and sophisticated of the group. For sheer poetic management of expression "Snel is Ons Lewe" (Swift is our Life), with its horse image, and "Hotel Aurora," a poem possessed, as it were, with the gloomy sound of bells in the night, are fine examples. Many of the poems, however, still have false, or partly false, applications; the poet's real interest is in the image, not the moral he reads into it. For Krige lacks as yet a subject on which the deeper forces of his nature can expend themselves.

He finds this subject at last in one poem—his long poem called "Lied van die Fascistiese Bomwerpers" (Song of the Fascist Bombers)—that is still one of the best things he ever wrote and is enough in itself to establish his reputation. The theme is the Civil War in Spain, and particularly the unprovoked bombing of Spanish civilians by the Fascists of the revolutionary Spanish Revolution who are aided by the "volunteer" air forces of Hitler and Mussolini. Their bombers laid waste in the name of the Roman Catholic Church and with the slogan on their lips that in the circumstances seems cruelly hypocritical: "Long Live Christ the King!" "Lewe Christus die Koning" is the refrain of their "Song," and Uys Krige uses and varies it as the poem goes on with increasing tragic and ironic depth.

This poem is full of passionate feeling that is expressed and controlled in the irony that blazes with rage, scorn, and indignation for the attackers, or with compassion for the victims. The rhythm and sound of the poem help to do many things at the same time—for example, they imitate the soaring and zooming of the airplanes, the gathering hum and drone of them, the sense of numbers swelling and swelling, of the noise swelling to a terrifying thunder. At the same time these technical devices imitate the joyous soaring and circling movements of the planes themselves; and this effect merges with a strong sense of the Spanish-Inquisition-like religious exultation of the men who kill so ruthlessly from their great height above the earth in the name of "Christ the King."

Then the movement of the bombs dropping from above is conveyed in an image suggesting not only the terror of the victims but the full moral horror of the deed; for the bombs are the black beads of a long rosary slipping through the blessed fingers of the bishops and the high priests as they patiently string them out, count them off, and slowly, one by one, drop them through the blue calmness of the day down towards the earth, on the cities, and the towns, and the farms. The force with which the poet communicates this moral horror grows and grows as the poem goes on, and one's sense of the evil, the unparallelled irony of the Fascist war-cry "Long Live Christ the King!" deepens. Most moving too is the way in which in a few lines Krige makes one feel how real are the ordinary people down below looking up with white, astonished faces, as they sit packed in trams, or picking red oranges in the citrus groves, or riding to market on their brown donkeys. As the poem ends, the cry from the airmen mounts as their bombs hail down and explode in vindictive triumph:

> Die, future! Die, hope!
> Die, love and compassion!
> Die, Spain!
> Live, Christ the King! [2]

It is impossible to give a proper idea of this poem without copious quotation, which for readers unlikely to know the language is fruitless. Suffice it to say that the poem is made of images startingly original and expressive, such as that of the rosary, or that of the airplanes of the enemy rising up out of the ruined cities like bluebottles out of a corpse. But most of these images lose half of their effect if translated, especially without their full context and their rhythm. It is a surprising feat of poetry that all the horror that the poem conveys is in the end subordinated to a sense of harmony, the harmony that is derived when, as Coleridge comments, beauty of form seems to strike out of the hardest truths of life like a conviction of its overwhelming value.

II *Die Einde van die Pad* and *Hart Sonder Hawe*

These two volumes of poems, the next in order of publication, are mainly about World War II; for, at about the time war broke out, Uys Krige felt that he could no longer identify himself with Afrikaner Nationalism because it had espoused the causes of Mussolini and Hitler, which he cordially hated. In 1940 he joined up, being sent North as a war-correspondent—a step that has cost him ever since his popularity with the majority of Nationalists and has earned him the cold shoulder from their critical press.

Die Einde van die Pad (The End of the Road) reflects, first, the poet's experiences just before the war; then the seemingly endless march through the desert, on the Somaliland border and in Abyssinia. It then moves to an American hospital, and finally to a hospital ship in the rain. *Hart Sonder Hawe* (Heart without Haven) takes up the tale, describing the mood of the army before the battle of Sidi Rezegh, where Uys Krige was captured. It then follows him to the prison camps of Tuturano and Fonte d'Amore, where he wrote some poems in English, which are included in the book; for he was surrounded there almost entirely, as he explains, by Englishmen and he began to think in English almost as much as in Afrikaans. At last *Harte Sonder Hawe* describes Mussolini's defeat and death; before the Germans could take over, Krige escaped from prison camp. The remaining poems in the volume were written at home in South Africa in the Low and the High Veld of the Transvaal and in the Cape—at Stellenbosch and elsewhere.

Most of the poems in *Die Einde van die Pad* express the weariness, the tedium, the anxiety, the gloom, the homesickness of soldiers in the earlier part of the North African campaign. They are all written in free verse, a form which Krige uses with skill and flexibility. There is a double kind of rhythm in all this verse: the rhythm which is built up, on the one hand, by the movement of the whole poem towards its denouément; on the other, that which paints what is happening during the journey, imitating in the curious way in which poetry can the movement in the mind, as it were, of thoughts and feelings or of sights and other sensations to suggest, say, the endless monotony of the desert, or the light, lively sparkling of a fountain, or rain falling softly on the softly sounding sea, or a thousand other things. Seldom does real poetry merely imitate sound, using onomatopoeia in the crude way one learned about at school; in suggesting sound, it also suggests half-a-dozen other things, faint traces of which in the memory—picked out of it for the reader by the words, sounds, and rhythm the poet uses—combine to create, in a peculiarly complex and delicate way, a strong sense of reality: the real is always complex.

There are still in a few of these poems faint marks of a straining after an application, a moral, which sometimes leaves a little snail-like trace of sentimentality at the end of them. But most are free of it. One of the best poems in the book is the first, "Waterkloof" dated August, 1939. A simple poem, it paints an idyllic day, as the poet and his wife, Lydia, and his baby daughter, Eulalia, lie in the early spring sunlight out on a high plateau. The poetry is alive: the images, especially the verbs, that make one see and feel sun, sky, and landscape, create a feeling of rapturous contentment that seems to quiver and glow like the light on the veld. Then a sound is heard "delicate and hesitant as the antennae of a butterfly": an airplane is approaching. The poet realizes the horror of what is probably coming to the world; yet, though the poem ends with the doubting prayer "Let it [the happiness] last long, O Lord, let it last long!," one is left with a conviction above all of the strength of this small human happiness—all the more so because it is so dreadfully threatened.

A poem that succeeds equally well is the one called "Blomme van die Boland" (Flowers of the Cape). In language grim as what it deals with, the poet describes a hideous place in the desert where, watched by vultures, the men have just finished knocking together a simple cross for a fallen soldier; it is made of a couple of loose planks from a petrol-case. The setting seems horrible: there is nothing to be seen but black lava rock, bare thorn trees and the desert, dirty-yellow everywhere like an old sore oozing pus. The thwart plank of the cross has scrawled on it in crooked black letters the name, date of death, number and unit of the dead man. The name is Jan van Niekerk, a typical Afrikaans-South African name—"such an ordinary name," says the poet, "exceptional only in the choice which the Gods have made for his grave. A soldier takes out a packet of "C to C" cigarettes,[3] out of which flutters a picture card which swirls about in the wind till it finally floats down face upwards on a piece of lava rock: it is a picture of four blue daisies playing in the wind, nodding above the grass.

By so simply, directly, and economically evoking the scene, the poet makes one feel, as if one were there, how in this most ugly, unhomelike waste there suddenly shines a presence—a presence that seems to incarnate, in its minute compass, home and everything about home that opposes what is about them. The blue daisy is seen everywhere in the Cape, when everything in the sudden, high jagged mountains and on the veld sown with millions of flowers is at its freshest and best. And the account of the picture card stabs into the reader's consciousness a pang for and an understanding of the homesickness of the men in this harsh, ugly place. The wind begins to blow the card about and then drops it, and it comes to rest against a soldier's boot. He bends slowly, picks it up, and puts it on the grave between the stones, then clambers back into the three-tonner, as the convoy grinds slowly into movement once more. Above the ash-grey grave as the convoy moves off, says the poet, the cross stands out clearly against the black lava-verge in the shuddering-white, blinding glow. And the poem ends with an invocation to the daisies to play in *this* wind and to nod above *this* earth.

It is a good poem—the economy of the language and the laconic rhythm express strongly and at the same time control the sadness of the longing and the death that is implicit in the simple episode. The effect when the picture card flutters down face upward is a little like that of the dead Cathy's sigh and her warm breath on Heathcliff's cheek as he tries to dig up her coffin in *Wuthering Heights*. Most of the poems in *Die Einde van die Pad* have something of the quality of this poem or of those to be found in the best poems of the two earlier volumes, although there is nothing here to equal "Lied van die Fascistiese Bomwerpers."

Harte Sonder Hawe is a much thicker collection of poems, many of which were written during Uys Krige's life in prison camps. A number of these poems are about his actual prisoner-of-war experience; and among these, especially among those written in English, are several failures. These are due to their being insufficiently thought out, like "The Taking of the Koppie," or to far too large a part of them being merely descriptive without sufficient point (like "The White Road"). A couple of the poems—"Ballade van die Krygsgevangene" (Ballad of the Prisoner of War) and "Before Sidi Rezegh" are marred by the use of inept dialogue. No one handles authentic Afrikaans dialogue better than Uys Krige, but when in "Ballade van die Krygsgevangene" he makes not an Afrikaner but an Italian guard speak in rather slangy, very ordinary Afrikaans, the mind does not accept it as genuine; and when in "Before Sidi Rezegh" he reports English dialogue, it rings false and is stiff and awkward; as a result, there is immediately a big hiatus in the reality of the poems. He would have done better to use *oratia obliqua*. Two of the English poems, "Midwinter" and "La Nebbia," are good. They have the kind of reality, the genuine human warmth, the truth of observation, and the total lack of affectation that stamp nearly all Uys Krige's work. But, though he does achieve poetry in English, his use of English almost never sparkles, ripples, and glows as his Afrikaans does with the sheer life of the language—the brilliance, the originality, the variety, and the flexibility of his own tongue at its best.

Among the remaining poems in the volume, most abandon utterly the wordiness of the bad poems from the prisoner-of-war camp. Instead many of them are rather short, many in very short lines and short stanzas which contain in narrow compass some passion and intensity, filling their container quite full. Three of those which I like best are "Hooglied" (Song of Solomon, literally High Song), "Verre Blik" (Far Vision), "Karroodorpie" (Karoo Village). The first sings of passionate love, as the poet thinks of his Maria, who, on a most lovely night of moonlight, slips off her clothes and washes her body in the waters of Helderberg[4]; then, says the poet,

> She steps into a swathe of darkness,
> And the blackest shadows glitter,
> She stands in a pool of light,
> And the moonlight itself is whiter,
> She hesitates between light and shadow,
> And that half-light begins to shiver.

The poetry manages to thow over this vision of Maria an aura of delight, like "the colouring of the imagination," or the moonlight.

The other two poems, in describing South African scenes with deep affection and even rapture, yearn for something worthier of them. In "Verre Blik" the poet communicates profoundly the glory and greatness, the golden peace and undisturbed vastness of the light and beauty of the landscape; and he ends by crying out to the people of his race, who despite everything that divides them, are still bound to his spirit, his soul, his heart: "Oh, *be* great and spacious and strong, be free, Full of light and quietness like this Southern land." "Karroodorpie" brilliantly imparts another aspect of the same feeling: as he contemplates the little village all alone in oceans of evening light—endlessness of golden heaven, golden earth—and the village there "Waiting for the first shadows, the evening star/So completely at one with this silence and rest," suddenly his heart is touched and a shuddering goes through his soul as he feels the pang of knowledge that he will never again be free of the division in himself: his country is so close to him, so much a part of himself; yet it is so foreign, so apart. The reader may imagine how much more, if Uys Krige felt this in 1943, he must feel it now.

"Swaels bo die Kamp" (Swallows above the Camp) acutely and feelingly expresses the homesickness of a prisoner-of-war watching the birds that may fly to his own home in his own far country, and his tenderness for his little daughter, Eulalia, left behind so long ago.

The poems after Lorca seem to fail; and one example is "Klaaglied vir die Kind Gewond deur die Golwe" (Lament for the Child Wounded by the Waves). They are, no doubt, a meritorious experiment, but such phrases as "die kind gewond deur die golwe" strike one as a kind of modernistic affectation: the child is not wounded; it is drowned. And, though the other images like "The child and its death terror, breast to breast/Were like two green spring rains entangled" are attractive sounding, they, too, strike one as obscure and affected. Why "spring rains"? The whole poem is, therefore, stifled by the fog of unreality they emanate.

Some of the adaptations have interesting imagery and a skillful use of verse forms, but all of them exaggerate. They aim at a sort of concentrated, naked intensity which one senses Uye Krige has not, in these contexts, actually experienced; and the poems lack,

therefore, what is usually this writer's chief source of strength—
his naturalness, directness, and reality.

III   *Vir die Luit en die Kitaar*

Unexpectedly enough the translations from Lorca succeed most
triumphantly in Uys Krige's next volume of poetry, a volume consisting entirely of translations, *Vir die Luit en die Kitaar* (For the
Lute and the Guitar [1950]).

I believe that translations of poetry ought to be judged without
reference to their originals. Because of the very nature of poetry,
it cannot be translated with entire success, for the combinations—
very subtle, delicate, and complex of intellectual meaning, sense-
impressions, sound, rhythm and associations that create poetic
meaning in one language—cannot possibly be exactly reproduced
in another. If, for example, the intellectual meaning can be conveyed in a word or with a phrase, it is most unlikely that the
sound will be right, and so on. The most that a translation can
hope to do is to make poems that can stand on their own feet as
poems. This Uys Krige hardly ever fails to achieve, and it is as
poems standing on their own feet that I propose to write of his
translations.

The first, and by a dozen pages, the longest of his translations,
"Kwatryne van Abu'l Ala" (Quatrains of Abu'l Ala), is, in my
opinion, the flattest of flat failures. It is apparently a very early
work, for two of the quatrains had appeared as independent
poems in *Kentering*. I fail to understand Uys Krige's enthusiasm
for this early Arab writer (born in 974 A.D.), who, judging by the
first of his *Opstelle* (Essays) at the end of the book, Krige prefers
to Omar Khayyam—at least as Fitzgerald presents him. The intellectual content of these sixty-eight interminable quatrains in this
translation is negligible; the tone, dreary, the manner, monoto-
nous; the poetry, thin and dry. There is a touch of rebellion
against the accepted that lends some interest, as in the last quat-
rain (I translate, for the sense alone):

> What's your belief? They rummage and admonish
> Another scans my genealogical tree.
> I am a son of God, the whole world is my tent,
> My race the human, till I find the grave.

But the whole is, in my opinion, not worth the labor of reading.

Of those poems translated from the French, the reverse is true. The verse translated is from Sully Prudhomme, Théophile Gautier, Delisle, Villon, Baudelaire, and Rimbaud—but the greater part of it is from Villon and Baudelaire. Certainly all the translations (except possibly the single Rimbaud, which I find too obscure to judge) stand firmly on their own feet as independent poems; all of them, often in very different ways, have the freshness of imagery and phrase, the variety, the music without which Uys Krige seldom writes. The best seem to be those from Villon and Baudelaire. Two particularly fine poems from Villon are "Grafskrif" (Epitaph) and "Ballade" (Ballad). Readers of Villon will know that he, with four other robbers, was condemned to death and wrote "Epitaph" in the expectation of being hanged. The translation is a complex poem: a delicate mixture of humility, pride, humor, grimness, piety, manly dignity, and self-mockery. It takes the cruel reality in its stride, investing it with these qualities. Consider, for example, the third verse, in which the poet describes the five corpses hanging, his own among them, as they will soon appear—washed clean by the rain; scorched black by the sun; their eyes pecked out by the crows; their heads nodding when the wind sighs, dancing when it roars. After each verse the refrain comes with a varying but most moving effect: "Maar bid die Heer dat hy genade gee" (But pray the Lord that he will mercy grant). We are stirred to compassion for the human lot. At the same time, the writer's poetic skill enchants us with the almost Chaucerian directness of its language and with the reality of images and pictures.

The same high degree of delicate complexity obtains in the translation of that prayer which Villon composed for his aged mother, "Ballade." The picture this poem gives us of the little old woman is moving. She is very old, with snow-white hair; she knows nothing and cannot read a syllable; but she is nevertheless "a faithful member of God's household." She humbly hopes and timidly yet serenely trusts that the Lord will grant her his grace. The poet strongly convinces the reader by subtle means of the happiness and strength this good old woman draws from her piety, which consists of her feeling that the concept of life that her faith contains gives her own life meaning and beauty. The refrain of her ballad runs: "In this so fair belief may I live and die." At

the same time, the poetry makes one conscious of her very essence
—one so different from Villon's yet treated by him with so much
understanding, love, and respect.

The Baudelaire translations also stand on their own feet as fresh
and strong as young trees. "Die Albatros" (The Albatross), for
example, consists of a single simile which compares poets to alba-
trosses; but it throws out its branches of intensely expressive language with vigor and precision. How the wonder of this "gigantic
sea-bird," this "prince of clouds, of space and sea," is felt and
communicated when "he sweeps among the stars and wakes the
wind," lurks in the tempest, and mocks the lightning! How, too,
quite as intensely, are his ridiculousness and ignominy conveyed
when he has been captured and drags and trails his huge wings
clumsily on the deck in absurd misery and comical ugliness. (Uys
Krige's Afrikaans here—as so often—is too excellently precise to be
translatable). And how sharply the point of the comparison is felt
—with the poet who soars with wide wings through his element;
but he is an exile in this world where his wings impede him as the
albatross's do.

Nearly all the translations from Baudelaire make excellent
poems. But perhaps the best poems of all in the book, certainly
the most powerful, are those translations from the Spanish Lorca—
most of them about the death of the bullfighter, Ignacio Sanchez
Mejias. Several of the other translations from the Spanish are fine,
too, notably the one from Lope de Vega, called "O Herder, wat
met Liefderik Gefluit" (Oh, Shepherd, who with Loving Flute). [5]
By the unselfconscious genuineness of its tone, this poem makes
one enter into religious feelings that one can only hypothetically
share.

There also are two from Lorca that are not about the death of
Ignacio. These two poems, "Dood van Antonito" (Death of Antonito) and "Ballade van die Rooi Vlag" (Ballad of the Red Flag)
are as striking in their way as the Ignacio poems. Both are written,
or, one should say, both are sung, in the traditional, surviving
Spanish ballad form; and, though both are obviously modern,
they use the same dramatic or poetic skills, and they sing out
clear, bright and bold as an ancient Scottish ballad like Sir Patrick
Spens. The images blaze with color and romance, the stories are
told with drama and passion, and the music and the dancing
rhythms of a guitar seem to strike out of them with full voice and

in a strong pattern. This poetry never hesitates or gropes. It seems to echo the proud heel-stamping, castanet-clicking vitality of the Spanish folk-measures, danced in movements by men so proud, manly and decided and by women so dashing; with hands clapped together and music shouted by a strong and tuneful voice.

Out of the poems made upon the death in the arena of Lorca's friend, Ignacio Sanchez Mejias, the bullfighter, Uys Krige has made four magnificent, if occasionally rather obscure, poems of his own. I do not often trust obscurity (like that of his Rimbaud translation). But the obscurity of the Lorca translations is in essence poetic. It is there because the images dare to leap the chasm from one association to another without weakening themselves by plodding out the distance between. This adds to the beauty an exciting power, and the effect is that of "a deep but dazzling darkness." For example, in the poem "Die Wond en die Dood" (The Wound and the Death), the wild grief and the dazed distraction of the speaker are suggested with the utmost intensity by the way the writer's attention fixes now on one thing and now on another: now on the everyday sight of life going on unchanged in the streets ("a child carrying a white sheet," "a basket of lime that has already been ordered"); now on nightmare associations with the hospital and First Aid ("The wind blew the wadding away", "And the whole arena was permeated with the iodine"); now on the symbol for life struggling with death ("already the dove and the leopard are fighting"); now on the bull, as he saw it storming down upon Ignacio. And beating through all this innumerable times—more and more insistently, louder and louder, like the merciless sound of a drum and like the relentless clang of the bells tolling for Ignacio's death, gathering power, drowning everything but the one thought, the realization of what has happened—comes the loud refrain: "Vyfuur in die middag" ("Five o'clock in the afternoon", the hour of the disaster). But the Afrikaans with its syllables strongly accented: "vyf," "uur," "mid" gives the effect far more powerfully than the English. The poem reaches a climax with the image of death laying its eggs in the wound, and the bells toll "Vyfuur in die middag/Vyfuur klokslag in die middag" (five o'clock on the stroke of the clock in the afternoon). And the word "klokslag" (with connotations in "slag" not only of striking but of a killing blow) suggests how the clock, like that in the

Housman poem,[6] collected all its multitudinous strength and struck Ignacio dead.

From this moment on, with the refrain still beating through it like a pulse in delirium, the grief seems to intensify more wildly, only now the poet, sparing himself nothing, is imagining how death feels to Ignacio: the sounds in his ears, "the bull bellowing behind his pale forehead"; "the corruption in his blood coming from afar"; "his wounds scorching like suns." And the poem ends as if with a shriek of anguish, as the drum-beat of the tolling bells pulses grimly through it,

> En die gepeupel breek die vensters
> Vyfuur in die middag
> Vyfuur in die middag
> O wat 'n vreeslike vyfuur in die middag.
> Dit was vyfuur op all die horlosies
> Dit was vyfuur in die skaduwee van die middag!

> (And the mob break the windows
> At five o'clock in the afternoon.
> Five o'clock in the afternoon.
> O, what a fearful five o'clock in the afternoon!
> It was five o'clock on all the watches!
> It was five o'clock in the shadow of the afternoon!)

It is interesting to see how here and in the poem as a whole the extreme passionate intensity of feeling is felt all the more because of the near rigidity of the formal construction: that one phrase "Five o'clock in the afternoon! " clamps down, as it were, on what is too humanly wild; and the form of the poem as a whole helps to distill music and beauty from pain.

Almost as fine, though marred by some obscurity, are the other three poems: "Die Uitgestorte Bloed" (The Poured-out Blood), "Die Liggaam Voor Ons" (The Body Before Us), and "Afwesige Siel" (Absent Soul); but, as it would take too long to analyze each in detail, only a few comments on each will be made. Each has so much power and suggests its own passion with music and imagery so striking, so original, so deeply felt that one cannot believe it is a translation: the words seem to come straight from the heart and mind of Ignacio's friend, as if he were freshly experiencing the horror and grief of the event. The emphatically repeated refrain of the poem about the bullfighter's blood poured out in the arena

("Die Uitgestorte Bloed")—"Ek wil dit nie sien nie" (I don't want to see it)—grows more and more horrified and insistent. But at the same time the speaker is forcing himself to see—to see the brilliant and manly greatness, the pride and fineness and courage of the man now gone forever, to picture in memory again his death and to realize fully what it meant to him, as he tries to climb the steps "with his whole death on his shoulders," as "he seeks for his steady profile, but a dream has misled him," as "he feels for his magnificent body, and he finds his streaming blood"—images which suggest, with powerful grief, the process of dying and the reluctance of the dying man to die. Finally the poet makes himself realize that for Ignacio, as he lies dead, with "the moss and grasses already opening with firm fingers the flower of his skeleton," and for himself, the poet, there is no comfort. Ignacio is dead; no song, no "torrent of carnations" can change that, "no glass can cover it with silver"—the funeral ceremony, the coffin and flowers, the consolations of Mother Church mean nothing—in that stark faith Ignacio died, and in it Lorca mourns for him.

"Die Liggaam Voor Ons" (The Body Before Us) is calmer, more somber, the grief is no longer so turbulent, but the rhythm and imagery, though less fevered, still suggest its whelming depth. The fact of the death permeates everything. The poet seems to be standing by the bier of his friend—here, he says, rests a stillness with the stench of death. Here he would like to see men with stentorian voices who tame horses and keep rivers within bounds, men with melodious skeletons who sing with mouths full of sun and firestones (flint)—here by this crushed torso of the captain bound hand and foot by death they would teach him a dirge like a deep river that would bear the blood of Ignacio away so that it might be lost without hearing that loud bellowing of the bulls. In these images, helped by sound and rhythm of which one cannot give an idea, a wonderful sense of the kind of man that the bullfighter was is called up; and, at the same time, the poet's longing for him not to be dead, not to have been gored to death by the bulls, is vividly present. The poem ends with a request that Ignacio's face should not be covered with a handkerchief to allow him to get used to the death that he bears. Go, Ignacio, says the poet, you will not feel again the warm bellowing. Sleep, vanish, rest: even the sea must die!

In "Afwesige Siel" (Absent Soul) the expressive music of the rhythm beats on the senses with a quieter but most sad, lamenting sound. The refrain of the first three verses, which deal with various things at home on the farm that will no longer know Ignacio, is "Want jy is dood vir altyd" (For you are dead for always). Then in the fourth stanza this is taken up as the poet mocks his friend in a chant like that of children chanting in "Schadenfreud," but exceeding the mockery is the bitterness of his acceptance of reality:

> For you are dead for always,
> Dead like all the dead of the earth.
> Like all the dead who are forgotten,
> Like a pile of dead mongrels in a heap.

Nobody will know you, says the poet, but I sing of your stature and your grace, the lofty maturity of your understanding, your hunger for death and the taste of his mouth, and the melancholy at the root of your manly joyousness. And the poem ends with the impression that such qualities do in their way get the better of death.

All these translations of the Ignacio poems give the impression of being very direct. Though their images strike into the heart, they glow with life and the language appears wonderfully spontaneous. Uys Krige says he wrote them almost straight off—he must have been in complete sympathy with Lorca. The excellence of his achievement lies in his having found Afrikaans words so precisely expressive of (apparently) every aspect of Lorca's meaning that a non-Spanish-speaker is convinced against all theory that the Afrikaans must be as good as the original Spanish.

IV *Ballade van die Groot Begeer*

Translating really good poems cannot but increase the translator's range and discipline in the use of his own tongue. Uys Krige, with his gift for languages, has translated many more poems, not yet collected, than appear in *Vir die Luit en die Kitaar*, notably some fine ones from Brazil which I have heard him read in his own inimitably rhythmic and almost possessed fashion. It is no doubt partly this salutary practice in translating writers as varied as Villon, Baudelaire, and Lorca that accounts for the very marked, consistent growth in originality, freedom, and strength that distinguishes his next (and so far his latest) volume of poems, *Ballade van die Groot Begeer* (Ballad of the Great Desiring).

These poems, in my opinion, are remarkable. They belong to the Cape Western Province, especially to the southern tip of it and to places like Paarl, Stellenbosch, Hermanus and their environs, and especially Cape Town. Their language is not, as in all Krige's other poems, that of a thoroughly educated, cosmopolitan Afrikaner; it is that of the Cape Colored people—a people of mixed blood, some of which is white, the rest African, Bushman, Hottentot—or very often Malay inherited from the slaves once imported to the Cape from Malaya. These people have for centuries been a part of western civilization quite as much as the white people have; they have never known a primitive tribal society like that of the Africans. Before Vervoerd, this fact was generally recognized in the Cape, where, for the "Coloureds" as they are called, there was no color bar in buses, trains, town halls, post offices, housing, and the like. But a color bar based on public opinion rather than on law or regulation did operate against them in other fields.

The Cape "Coloureds" are nearly all Afrikaans-speaking, but for the mass of them it is Afrikaans with a difference: an Afrikaans with English words and corruptions of English words freely mixed in, as well as a sort of slang of the slums, where large numbers of the "Coloureds" live. There are exceptions, of course. Some "Coloureds" speak a pure Afrikaans—I know one old woman who was so conservative that she favored High-Dutch forms of certain words. But most Cape Town "Coloureds" use such words as "pêllie-blou" (pronounced "pally-blow") which presumably is made up of the English "pal" and the Afrikaans "blou" meaning blue, here as in "true blue"; "jop" (pronounced "yawp") is a corruption of the English "job," and so on. Some pronunciations are peculiar to the "Coloureds"; for example, for "jy" and "jou" (pronounced "yay" and "yow," as in bow and arrow, many of them say "djy" and "djou" (pronounced "jay" and "jow").

Uys Krige knows firsthand this language and its people. A poet and dramatist naturally does a great deal of loafing and apparently

aimless talking in low places as well as high—that is how he gets
to know people—and Uys Krige has done his share of it. And by
writing in their kind of language Krige has added a new kingdom
to Afrikaans. He also in these poems exercises his gift for a truly
dramatic kind of dialogue—one that expresses with delicacy and
subtlety yet unmistakably the character and personality of the
speaker with nuances that could hardly be conveyed and could
certainly not be "carried alive" into another mind by pages of description.

The Cape "Coloureds," as a group, do have a distinctive character of their own. Poverty, disease, injustice, drink, dagga,[7] vice,
promiscuity, the consciousness of being looked down upon by the
whites—nothing seems to quench their vitality. When down, they
bound up again; their spirits are high, their wit ready, their impu-
dence disarming. Much given, like most slum people,[8] to crime
and drink, they are nevertheless tough and full of courage and
humor, with the gift of dramatizing and enjoying heartily their
precarious existence. In private life, they are born actors; and,
when they take to dancing, they move with grace and élan. Several of them have made names for themselves at Covent Garden
and elsewhere.

All the poems in this volume except the last "Lied van die
Lamp" (Song of the Lamp), are put into the mouths of Colored
people—or spoken, as it were, out of their being, so imaginative is
their creation. Consequently, the book is a wonderfully gay book,
even when the seamy side of life is being most graphically dealt
with, as in "Loflied" (Song of Praise). This poem about the notorious and dreadful Cape Town slum, Windermere, dances and
shuffles along with a cheerful, mocking, relentlessly clear-sighted
irony and with not a trace of self-pity. Most of the poems in *Ballade van die Groot Begeer* are real ballads in one of the oldest
senses of the word—they are meant to be sung and danced to, in
this case to the kind of banjo, guitar, or concertino music that
the "Capeys" (as they are often called) love. How successful Uys
Krige has been in achieving this effect is shown by a story that he
told me himself. One day a friend of his heard a great deal of
happy music going on in a stationary truck full of Colored men:
she looked in to see what it was all about. There on the floor of
the truck was spread out a double page of the *Weekend Argus;*

printed on it was one of Krige's "Capey" poems that had just appeared, and the Colored men were busy improvising a tune and dance to his words. The poet was naturally delighted.

The poem in question was the scintillating "Klopsdans" (Club Dance—klops, pronounced "klawps"—being a corruption of the English word "club." The clubs in question are a great feature of Cape Town life. They are essentially music clubs, and every New Year's Day and the day after a great festival is held on Green Point Common. There the clubs sing, dance, and act little scenes with strange remnants of Malayan and Javanese ceremonies in them. They are called strange names like "The Modest Violets" or "The Yellow Tigers," and they wear gorgeous blazers in blazing colors; their supporters wear "coon" costumes of brilliant satin, with top hats to match. As they compete for prizes, they try to outdo one another in extravagance, and the whole of Cape Town is filled with dancing, singing, capering, happy Colored people (often with collection boxes). It is so gay that the more sedate whites can't help being infected with the carnival spirit. The festivity comes to a head on the first and second of January, both holidays in the Cape. After that it slowly peters out; but for another three or four weeks groups of "coons" are found wandering about the streets in their gaudy satin clothes, singing, playing their banjos and their drums, and still sometimes shaking their collection boxes. Perhaps the greatest gift the gifted "Coloureds" have is their unquenchable vitality, their gift of enjoying themselves. "Klopsdans" conveys this quality above all—and with feeling and artistry.

The poem is in the form of a sort of dramatic monologue, spoken or hummed or sung by one of the club men, and it is interrupted at intervals by an objector. The first speaker communicates, with sparkling vividness, the sense of the whole city overwhelmed and charmed by this laughing and dancing sea of "Coloureds." Cape Town is ours today, he says, we are the lions of it, not Lion's Head, nor the lion at Groote Schuur.[9] His rhythms suggest the shuffling, whirling, winding, twisting, bounding, leaping rhythm of the people dancing along the streets; the happy twanging of the banjos and guitars; the beat of the dancing drums; and the lift and extravagant overflowing of the light heart. As he prances along, the speaker hails friends and acquaintances, makes advances to pretty girls, chatters and laughs and exults.

The interrupter tries his best to dampen the other man's spirits by reminding him of how drunk he will be by dawn tomorrow; how the police will probably pick him up and throw him into the pick-up van; how the home he creeps into at night—if he gets home—is a miserable hole; how he is oppressed by the white people; how his vote has been taken away from him. But the dancer is far too happy even to hear him. The poem ends with his telling the interrupter not to mutter so inaudibly but to join in the dance. He lends him his colored top hat, tells him he is now a club member too, and advises him to cut in and set his feet chopping and shuffling with the rest. Unable to resist the music and the spirit of the carnival once he has taken five steps, the interrupter is presently dancing too, along with the "slêppie-hêppie" crowd. After all, says he, in time to the music, I too am a child of the sewers. And so, through speaker and interrupter, the whole poem gives us a subtle, many-faceted idea not only of the "coon carnival," as they call it, but of the way most of the "Coloureds" live in Cape Town and of the kind of people they are.

The book is full of poems that extend just as successfully an idea of these people (and so, of course, of life). A delightful one in which humor and genuine pathos are exactly mingled is "Skietgebed van die Skollie" (Hurried Prayer of the Skolly—a "skolly" is a Cape-Colored word for a young tough or hooligan; "skietgebed" means literally "shot-prayer"—a prayer shot off in haste and fear, at gun-point, as it were). Uys Krige's warmth and understanding and his poet's complete fellow feeling with the skolly permeate the poem without damaging his knowledge of the impermanence of this hurried repentance. The poem is a prayer to "Baas Jesus" (Boss Jesus)—Krige reflects in many poems the religion which these people have been taught and do not question. The skolly is waiting in the dock. The Judge ("die Juds"—a corruption of judge, pronounced "yuds") has not yet come in and the skolly is in a state of terror at the thought not so much of prison but of the cane or cat-o'-nine-tails. (His crime has been one of drunken violence, and he is in danger of the lash.) Not far away sits his mother, a kind, good woman who has done her best to bring him up properly. The refrain of the prayer to Jesus to spare him prison and the cuts is "Al is dit nog om harentwil, O Heer"—"Even if it is only for her sake, O Lord."

As the poem progresses, the skolly thinks of the happy, irre-

sponsible, drunken deeds that he has so much enjoyed and that
have led him to this plight. He hardly even knows what he has
done. He's kicked in his friend's ribs, apparently, but all he remembers is that Jan was flirting with his "Lollie-pop," his floosie,
his "Dollie-losbol." He makes excuses for himself—he is not the
worst; the Judge himself is said to have strayed from the path of
righteousness at times. But, as the Judge's appearance grows more
and more imminent, he becomes more and more conscious of how
much the flogging is going to hurt, with "weals deep and red and
raw" and his prayer becomes more urgent.

Suddenly the court grows still; the Judge arrives; how stern his
face is! The skolly makes desperate promises to "Baas Jesus" to
reform. And, as his own anguish of anxiety sharpens, he becomes
more and more aware of his mother sitting in the court room;
finally his terror for himself at the thought of the agony that will
be inflicted on him merges into pity for her—a real deep pang of
grief—and into remorse at being the cause of her suffering. Think
of my mother, he says to Jesus, how weak she is, how faint. The
refrain "Al is dit net om harentwil, O Heer" intensifies and grows
more unselfish—though there is an even clearer ironic consciousness that the Lord's sparing his mother means that he will be
spared too.

In the last verse the rhythm is rapid and panicky. The skolly
sees the tears stealing down his mother's grey cheeks, and hur-
riedly he begs Jesus to think of *his* mother. A mother's love, he
says (and for the moment he feels it absolutely)—what more does
one want? But how much he is thinking of himself is shown by the
terrified idea that interrupts his musing on mother love. "Daai kat
se stert, dit slaat jou bafta-blou" (That cat's tail, it hits you purple-
blue). Panic-stricken, he turns to the mother of God herself. She
at least, being a mother, can be counted on to be merciful; she
may intercede for him. And the poem ends with two lines both
touching and amusing

> O, help my, mammie van die Lam, gou! gou!
> Al is dit net om harentwil, O Heer!
> (Oh, help me, mammy of the Lamb, quick! quick!
> Even if it's only for her sake, O Lord!)

But it is impossible in another language to do justice to the
humor, knowledge, pathos, and insight of this poem.

The Poems

A beautiful ballad has been made out of an old anecdote that dates from the Spanish influenza epidemic of 1918. In Cape Town and in other places this plague raged almost as fiercely as the Black Death in London in Pepys's time. I remember that in the small town of Stellenbosch where I then lived, three hundred people died every week of the *grippe* ("griep" or "pes" as it was called); and, in the much larger city of Cape Town with its terrible slums, the death rate was so high that at one time a death cart passed through the streets every day to bear the coffins of the newly dead to the graveyards. Krige's poem, "Swart Oktober" (Black October) tells a story of which the following is a rough outline: The death cart is rattling through the empty sunlit streets of Cape Town on a beautiful spring day in October. There is no other sound. Two broken-down nags are pulling the cart, their knees almost giving under them. On the driver's seat sits Frans Pieterse, cheeky as a bantam cock—but there is the mark of fatigue on his sharp face. In a narrow side street he comes upon a man sitting on the edge of the pavement, all shrunk together, his dull eyes fixed on the ground. Frans recognises his old friend Koos, and hails him: "You're sick," he says; "Why aren't you in your bed?" "There are nine sick people and it's very dark there," says Koos. "And I'm going to die [he uses the coarse word "vrek" —pronounced "frak"—which is ordinarily applied only to animals] even though I am as tough as a badger. Yes, I'm going to die, I know that well, and if I must die, I'll die here in the sunlight just in the street." "Excellent," cries Frans, "that's my Koos as I know him—that's the language for that mug of yours, a mug of mugs!" And he cracks his whip to go. But, when he sees his friend's head fall forward as if he has really at last fallen to pieces, he says, "Can I do anything for you?" Frans looks a bit less dashing, even a little upset. But Koos tells him to fetch his coffins, or the poor corpses will never be buried, and to bring him, perhaps, a rose.

The death cart disappears. The street sinks into absolute silence again. The sick man sighs, his head sinks to his knees, but he takes comfort from the sun. Presently the rattling of the death cart is heard again, and Frans appears with a new load of coffins, big and small, black and brown and yellow (these colors suggest the races of the people who have died). Koos is full of pity when he sees a very small one; and Frans, seeing how deathly sick he is, and being pretty sick himself, sings out: "Climb up, old friend! Climb into the Churchyard Express: I won't have time to fetch you to-morrow! " Koos struggles and groans and sweats, but he manages to get up; and Frans affectionately pulls him towards himself to lean against his chest and make himself comfortable. Off they go; and the street is chalk white and shadowless again, and in the distance at Roggebaai (Rye Bay) the sea washes silver on the shore. There is a strong suggestion, of course, that both men will be dead by the time the cart gets to the burial-place.

I despair of explaining why this poem makes such a strong impact of beauty because the secret lies largely in the language. It gives a much more vivid idea than any account can hint of the gaiety and recklessness and ironic acceptance and cheerful endurance of life's hardships and horrors that form so large an element in the courage of these two dying old men. They take miseries for granted; and, even in such traits as this, their humor is not to be repressed: the death cart with both of them soon to be dead in it is mocked at with the name, "The Graveyard Express." And Koos, for example, speaks with neither awe nor self-pity of his own coming death: he is going to "vrek," the same process that a dog or an ox goes through. The secret also lies in such images as that which Koos uses, and which permeate the poem, of the sound of the death cart being like the tokkel-tokkel of a guitar—a spirited note, they shall have music on their funeral journey.

As much as anything, the effect of this poem lies in the delightful sense one is infected with the sweetness of that life which these two men are leaving, and of which the Plague, "like a beach hyena" (for we are made aware throughout the poem of the sea that washes the shores of Cape Town), is robbing and has robbed many thousands of people. This realization of life's sweetness enters deeply into one's being when the poet describes the beauty of Cape Town and the beauty of the day. Throughout the ballad, in a sentence here and a phrase there in the midst of the action, one is made to feel as if one were there in the tranquil loveliness of the deserted city, so beloved by these two men, as it lies empty and clean, its buildings white and yellow. The air is like the flame of a blue-white turquoise, Table Bay is a-glitter like a diamond, the arum lilies are white on the slopes of Table Mountain and the vygies[10] preen themselves on Signal Hill. The whole city stands in a soft flame of light, the spring day is gentle on Frans's neck as the down of a dove, and the light rests like bloom on everything. The city is absolutely quiet; and, though the Plague roams about like a wolf, slinking from door to door to tear and tear with its fangs, it is noiseless. All is silent. There is not even a cat or a dog in the streets. You might be in the veld rather than in a town.

These details are scattered throughout the poem so that their effect pervades it subtly, just as the light smell of mountain pines mingled with that of sea is wafted through the city with the sunlight in which it is gently steeped. The result is that the mind is lifted above the purely human and anecdotal qualities of the poem into an awareness of the greatness and mystery—the beauty, it seems—beyond mere human life.

There are many other fine poems. The one after which the volume is called, "Ballade van die Groot Begeer," is the song of a "Capey" tortured and plagued all his life by insatiable desire, first for a doll, then for a top, then drink, then dagga, then for one woman after another, then for the status of being white. But at the bottom of all his desires is the bitterness of self-knowledge: the refrain of the poem runs, "O, kom daar nooit 'n einde aan die Groot Begeer" (Oh, will there never be an ending to the Great Desiring?). In the Envoy, he prays to "Prince Jesus": if by some extraordinary but not impossible grace, he is ever taken up to Heaven when he dies, will there be even there, he begs doubtfully, an ending to the Great Desiring? The situation is felt with complete reality, and the language is as lively as if the man were standing breathing before one.

One or two poems at most are not much more than anecdotes, but usually they have been turned into something more. "Vignette" is about a Colored woman who is riding home in a crowded bus; her baby, though it is his feeding-time, is too sleepy to suck at the naked breast she offers him while she laughs and chats loudly to her friends. At length, in desperation, she sets the whole bus, including the one white woman on it, shouting with laughter by threatening the baby that, if he doesn't take it, she'll give it to the "guard" (she uses the English word). The story is so told that it seems to epitomize the gregarious enjoyment of life at which the "Coloureds" are so adept.

This effect is produced partly by the writer's good humor that warms everything like the summer sun (it is a summer afternoon), and partly by the way one is made aware of the fullness of the bus, the tough patience of the white conductor, his good-nature and helpfulness, the turbulence of the happy drunks, the "warm" music of the youth's guitar, the robustness of the mother with her naked breast "brown and shining and heavy and full and round," the sleepiness of the baby who seems warm and happy and full like his mother's breast, the sociable chatter and gossip and laughter and the frank language that fills the vehicle. It is effective partly because gently suffusing everything is the sense of the Cape Town summer lying all around—a full, ripe summer that "gleams about us in ten-thousand vineyard leaves," the "harvest-time," that as the poem goes on becomes warmer, later and more languid, as "the vineyards lie wide about (the roads) and bake in the sun." Everything in the poem suggests the ripeness and richness of life, and at the same time it is an extraordinarily faithful picture of a local feature, an aspect of Cape Town life, the bus crowded mostly with "Coloureds" going home.

Many of the poems are about fish, fishermen, and the sea of this Cape of Storms. The very first poem in the book is called "Vishoring" (Fish Horn) and another is "Gekraakte Klarioen" (Cracked Clarion)—both titles refer to the horn that the fish hawkers blow as their little carts clatter through the streets of such places as Cape Town, Stellenbosch, and Paarl to summon the housewives with their welcome but raucous note. "Vishoring," a little jewel of a poem, sparkles and dances with high spirits, catching in its net all kinds of things: the exact tone and accent of the vendor's "Capey" Afrikaans, the tone of his relationship with the white "Merrem," [11] with the Colored servants, with the urchins who try to filch his fish; the lightness and brightness of the morning, with the sun and the sea breeze in it; the glorious beauty and the freshness and variety and plenty of the fish that lie shimmering in the vendor's cart like rainbows; even his love of watching rugby football (the colors of the fish remind him of rugby blazers); and his simple kind of Christianity, half-sincere, half-conventional and expressed with humor and originality. All these impressions are given in rhythms extremely light-footed; for, as the hawker says, his heart can hardly help bounding for joy.

More somber are the poems about the sea; for examples, there are "Gebed vir die 'Silwer Koor'd" (Prayer for the "Silver Cord") and "Ken jy die See" (Do you know the sea?). Both poems are about the hazards of the fisherman's life. Uys Krige has lived a great deal near the sea, and because of the ease with which he falls into intimate conversation with people everywhere, high or low, white or Colored, he has got to know the people who live by venturing out over the deep even in uncertain weather, so as to be able to catch enough fish for their families to keep body and soul together. The casualty rate is high. "Ken Jy die See?" has been outstandingly successful among all kinds of people. Krige has had many letters about it, one of them about how it had been read aloud at the funeral of some drowned fisherman and had greatly moved the congregation.

In this poem, the refrain, slightly varied, states after each stanza, as refrains should with deepened significance, "Dan sê jy nog, Meneer, die vis is duur" (Then you still say, Sir, the fish is dear). Without quotation from the original, it is impossible to give any idea of the immediacy of the language with which Uys Krige describes the terrors of a storm at sea for those who are struggling in a frail fishing boat against the unimaginably huge powers of the elements. I give one example, which I can only lamely and literally translate into prose—rhyme and rhythm I must do without:

> Was jy al van jou bootjie soos 'n veer gevee
> Deur 'n grys golf hoog soos die tronk se muur?
> Wat help dit on te spartel en te skree 'Nee! Nee!'
> Sluk jy eers daardie waters sout en suur?
>
> (Have you ever been swept from your little boat like a feather
> By a grey wave high as the wall of a gaol?
> What use is it to flounder, struggling, and to cry "No! No!"
> Once you swallow those waters salt and sour?)

This is only one of many poems in the volume which does for the poor or oppressed in South Africa the most useful service that can be done for them—which, voicing no ideology and recommending no political panacea, yet makes one feel (not merely say, but feel and realize) the fact that each man is the center of his own universe and therefore as important to himself as any other man is to himself. This awakening of the imagination in all his readers is a writer's special gift to his generation, and Uys Krige has made it available to his countrymen.

There has been it becomes clearer and clearer, since *Kentering* appeared in 1935 a steady and decided growth in originality, range, and poetic skill in Uys Krige's poetry. His insight now goes far deeper than it used to; experience enables him to understand the heart more fully and to catch more exactly the tone of voice, choice of words, and turn of phrase of a group of people whom he has grown more and more to admire. He has also learned to economize, to discipline his muse more; his rhythms have become even more expressive; and his control of the resources and potentials of his own language has strengthened to catch, especially in this volume about the Cape "Coloureds," eloquent innovations. *Ballade van die Groot Begeer* is unquestionably his best book of poems to date.

CHAPTER 8

The Short Stories

UYS KRIGE has published only two volumes of short stories, *Die Palmboom* (The Palm Tree) and *The Dream and the Desert*. An interval of nearly twenty years separates the writing of some of them, for *Die Palmboom* was published by van Schaik in 1940 and *The Dream and the Desert* was published by Collins of London in 1953. *Die Palmboom* is in Afrikaans; *The Dream and the Desert*, in English.

Of the nine stories in *Die Palmboom*, three of them—"La Miseria," "Die Skaapwagter met sy Wolmussie" (The Shepherd and his Woollen Cap), and "Die Feejuffertjies van Reyniers" (The Fairy Misses of Reyniers)—are from folklore, Spanish and French. The last of these has a touch of sentimental prettiness, but the other two canter with a born storyteller's gusto in sparkling Afrikaans, full, fluent, and lively. The rest are all about South Africa. " 'n Seun word Gebore" (A Son is Born) uses the imagination at a greater depth than any of the others. The scene is a Voortrekker lager in the Drakensberg, just after the still unguessed-at treachery of Unghunghunghlovu, where Dingaan massacred Piet Retief and all his men, who had come at Dingaan's invitation to conclude a treaty with him. A girl is contentedly expecting the birth of her first child; the lager is attacked; she escapes to warn another camp; and her child is born that night. Though this story has nothing like the dramatic and emotional force of a similar episode in Krige's *Magdalena Retief*, where scene after scene has already built up reality and suspense, the tale does not lack fine qualities. The lovely encampment in the Drakensberg, the everyday life there, the women beating out the washing on rocks, brothers and sisters teasing one another, the golden happiness of Maria's mood—all are conveyed with freedom and freshness of observation. Unfortunately, the contrast with the horror soon to break loose is rather muffed by half a paragraph of narration where there should be action; and the reader is let down for a moment out of life into the history books.

This fault—of telling the story instead of making it happen— mars the story called "Die Palmboom" and most of "Die Uitkoms" (The Solution). Perhaps the most successful story in the book is "Die Diefstal" (The Theft), of which the scene is laid in Stellenbosch. A little boy (obviously the author's brother François, now an artist of note), enchanted by the illustrations, steals a book from Darter's Bookshop (now defunct); and his point of view and behavior, and those of his brothers and friends, are described in language which at once truthfully reflects, heartily sympathizes with, and laughs at them. "Die Stad" (The City), about another little boy, is real too, but it is only a slice of life in which the details don't make enough of a design. The book as a whole, though in Afrikaans (Krige's right hand), is imagined with far less depth of experience and written with far less skill than his *The Dream and the Desert,* which is in English, Krige by this time having become almost ambidextrous.

The title of *The Dream and the Desert,* though attractive, is something of a misnomer. The book contains the nouvelle "The Dream"; of the remaining eight items listed in the table of contents, only two are about the North African desert, or, rather, the war in it: "The Death of the Zulu" and "Two Daumiers." The one-acter which concludes the volume is the latest version, this time in English, of a play already discussed in another chapter, *Alle Paaie Gaan na Roma.* Though about the war, the events of the story happen in Italy, and the same is true of "The Charcoal Burners" and "The Christmas Box." As for "The Invisible Shepherd," it is frankly a French folk or fairy tale, the same that appeared in Afrikaans in *Die Palmboom* under the title of "Die Skaapwagter en Sy Wolmussie"; and "La Miseria" (Spanish for "Poverty") is a Spanish folk tale, which also is repeated. This is the story of the old woman who captured Death when he stuck to her orange tree— the self-same tale on which a large part of *Die Goue Kring* is based. The remaining story, "The Coffin"—the best in the book next to "The Dream"—is set in South Africa; and, like "The Dream," it is partly autobiographical.

The two desert stories are, as it happens, the least successful in the volume; but one of them, "The Death of the Zulu," has won more acclaim, possibly, than any other tale in the book. Such stories are popular because of the presence in them of that ingredient which the world, in its present miserable stage of the development of civilization, falls down before and worships, whether from the Left or the Right—namely, self-consciousness about color. It seems almost impossible for anyone, white or black to think in 1964, much less to write, objectively about this problem; but its mere presence in a work of art creates an excitement that people attribute (according to whether they agree or disagree with the writer's sentiments) to the excellence, or else to the badness of his artistry. There is only a trace of this self-consciousness in the two stories, yet it has no doubt contributed to their being preferred to work of finer quality.

"The Death of the Zulu" is about a Zulu soldier of magnificent physique, whom the narrator finds mortally wounded after the Battle of Sidi Rezegh, when he and the Zulu are both, though they hardly realize it as yet, prisoners-of-war. The Zulu is in such agony that he begs the narrator over and over again, in Zulu, to shoot him. The South African cannot bring himself to do this, nor can the German medical officer. Finally the medical officer orders a combatant soldier to do it; it is done, and the story ends. This is a good piece of reportage but nothing more.

"The Two Daumiers" is also good reportage. Two war-correspondents are discussing whether the horrors they are going to view after a battle are like Goya or Daumier. They decide that Goya is too romantic, and presently they come upon a subject fit for the dryer pencil of Daumier, for it cannot be romanticized. Krige here paints an unforgettable picture of what has happened to the bodies of two men when the top was blown off their tank. The second Daumier is of the corpse of a young Basuto from Mokhotlong whom the correspondents had met earlier that day brimming over with ebullience and the delight of being about to be given a rifle to fight with. The South African government has forbidden the issue of rifles to Africans in the forces, but the army has disagreed—at least as far as Basutos are concerned. This story surpasses the more popular "Death of the Zulu" because it is illuminated by more of those gleams of reality and human insight that are to be found in nearly everything Uys Krige writes.

Why should these two stories strike one as being touched with self-consciousness about the color bar? The touch, after all, leaves hardly a trace. Perhaps it is because it is so difficult for a white person to think or feel with any confidence about the Africans he lives with. With the Colored people, it is quite a different matter—they are a part of white civilization. When white people are concerned with civilization, they can write—and read—with a certain amount of confidence. They know, comparatively, much about it from introspection and from the huge literature in many languages that has interpreted it for them—it is, to a certain degree, familiar ground. But, in the case of the Africans, there is no indigenous literature—nothing one can read—to help the whites. They can know the blacks from the outside, but the blacks themselves have not revealed themselves even to themselves in literature. And without the enormous quantity of first-hand knowledge that literature provides (for every writer tells one essentially about himself, drawing on his self-knowledge to understand others), the whites are at something of a loss. Noni Jabavu's *Drawn in Colour* is an invaluable help but it is only one book; the whites need many more—and many from people less westernized than she. That there are great differences between the inherited ideas and feelings of the two races in South Africa seems undeniable; and this difference must cripple the confidence of white writers trying with full seriousness to interpret the minds of black people. Only the shallowly confident win an easy fame.

Nobody could read "The Charcoal Burners" or "The Christmas Box," without being moved—to grief, in the first case—for these and many other Italian partisans caught and executed after deeds of the utmost bravery and kindness; to pity and admiration, in the second, for the courage with which horribly mutilated soldiers bear their afflictions. "The Christmas Box," about a hospital ward full of mutilated men, shocks one to tears by making one feel the courage of a faceless and probably dying Indian, so horribly deprived that one would long for him to die, but for the vitality and fellow feeling that he still somehow manages to express.

"The Charcoal Burners," told in leisurely fashion by a South African ex-prisoner-of-war who describes his escape to the Canadian forces in Italy after the fall of Mussolini, seems steeped, like *The Way Out,* in golden light that is partly sunlight—partly something generous, brave, and romantic in the people it concerns. All through the story one is made keenly conscious of the mountain country in which it all happens, of the people who seem so akin to that sunny grandeur, the three charcoal burners: Arturo, the dwarf; his gigantic son, Pietro; and Pietro's lover, Mariana, for whom no priest will venture up the mountain through the German and Fascist forces to make her Pietro's wife. The life they live high up the mountain slope, hunting deer for their food, all proud and happy in themselves and one another, is like an idyll; and as the story approaches its end, the reader's heart beats with anxiety lest all this should be lost (as it is) by the very qualities that create the beauty—the humanity, the daring, the unstinted generosity. Uys Krige is in such stories as these certainly paying that debt to the peasants of the Abruzzi

> . . . that a grateful mind
> By owing owes not, but still pays, at once
> Indebted and discharged.[1]

But by far the best stories in the volumes are "The Coffin" and "The Dream." "The Coffin" is about the Lourens family, Uys Krige's forebears on his father's side. The story happens on a farm in the Swellendam district (Cape), Bontebokskloof, belonging to Petrus Lafras Lourens, great-grandfather to the narrator. The tale begins on the day the narrator is born in the old farmhouse, and it ends many years later on the day the old man dies. As in all Krige's stories, the lovely landscape in which the story is set permeates the tale as much as any of the characters do. Felt like powerful presences are the old man and his wife—the old man who is alive with the love of life and with individuality, caprice and humor until the last moment of breath; who commands all about him by natural force of character; and who, in his power of endurance, the dignity with which he hides his suffering, and the warmth and magnanimity of his mind, has a kind of greatness of soul which the circumstances of his life have helped to breed. The old woman —whose sex prevents her from developing (even if she otherwise could or wished to) the exuberance and extravagance which partly his position as patriarch causes to flourish in the interesting old man—commands with peculiar quiet strength herself. An example of her power is the following:

On other occasions his mood was warm and human, full of understanding—gentle as sunlight on green hills after rain. Sometimes, however, it became boisterous, extravagant. Then his laughter would come in great gusts of bawdy humour; he would be so forthright, so exuberantly coarse that many of us, especially the older ones, would have tears running down our cheeks and Great Ouma, if she were present, would lift up her hands as if to ward off a blow, and then quietly, but very effectively put an end to all this "godlessness." It was then I always felt his humour was vital and earthy; and it had something physical like sea-water streaming over you on a hot summer's day and making your whole body tingle with coolness.

The story is a triumph of the creative imagination, for the tale is seen through the eyes of a small boy. It seems very closely related to the lovely "Dream," especially because the image of Cancer, "the crab," which haunts "The Dream," is clearly seen here. The image first occurs in the following passage:

One afternoon I was walking along the riverbed, about two miles from the homestead. There, in a desolate kloof against the mountain, I was startled by a weird protracted sound from somewhere nearby. It stopped, then began again. It was like a long drawn-out groan; that of an animal, I thought, in great pain. I had come to a dead stop, listening. Then I walked forward mechanically and, forcing my way through some undergrowth, came upon Great Oupa sitting on a grassy bank. He was bending over with his hands clenching his knees. On his contorted face there was an expression I shall never forget; and while he clenched and unclenched his hands, fierce groans broke from his lips.

A cold hand seemed to touch my heart. Then Great Oupa noticed me where I stood, bewildered and speechless, beside a shrub.

At once the agonised expression had disappeared, the face was normal again, the gaze calm and the eyes had the first little spark of a smile. He beckoned to me. I sat down beside him. Within a few minutes he was as amusing as ever, telling me about the good old days when he and his three brothers were small boys; how they practically lived down here in the river-bed; how with enormous guns that to-day would kick grown-up people clean out of their boots, they had hunted wild animals, yes, even leopards, all on their own, here, in this same tangled kloof.

But I had a strong feeling something was wrong and I could hear my heart throbbing. Beads of sweat, I noticed, stood on Great Oupa's forehead; and now and again his fingers would tremble slightly.

We walked through the veld. Great Oupa was still talking animatedly; and as he talked, he would flick off the head of a veld flower with his horse-whip, something I had never seen him do before.

At table that evening he was as humorous as ever. But I did not sleep much that night.

The feeling of fear and horror, the cruel assault on my young mind and imagination that I had experienced that afternoon in the kloof, was repeated with shattering immediacy when a few months later I learned in one of my first Latin lessons that the word cancer meant 'crab.'

This episode is so told that the mere mention of the word "crab" at the end of it makes us imagine, all too vividly, the progress of the disease.

Fortunately, readers may all read "The Dream" for themselves. Though in English, it seems the best of Uys Krige's prose tales. The story of a twelve-year-old boy's first horrified skirmish (when his baby brother dies) with the realization of death, the tale creates the world of a small boy of sturdy and agile physique, who lives largely for playing and watching rugby football, as well as playing other boisterous games like "Kick and Jump." He is gregarious and boisterous, but is also pursued by scientific ardor. The boy is not merely an extrovert, however; he responds to all aspects of life with warmth of sensibility and imagination; and the world created is not merely experience as apprehended by a boy, it is also this solid, this "much-loved earth" and in particular one corner of it which I, his critic, know almost as well as the writer—the town of Stellenbosch in the Cape Western Province—Stellenbosch built in the angle made by blue jagged mountains, with the piny hill, Pappegaaisberg, on the remaining side; its streets shaded by huge, ancient oaks; the mountain water, crystal clear, clattering down the deep pebbled furrows in their shadow. Part of the story takes place in Claremont, a suburb of Cape Town built among still bigger and more numerous oaks and with roaring stone pine woods climbing behind the houses part-way up the slopes of Table Mountain. A lovelier corner of the world is rarely to be found, and Uys Krige has recreated it with a skill that will delight those who don't know it almost as much as those who do. Many of the people in this world are real, like the landscape, in two senses —that they are portraits of people who lived there thirty or forty years ago, and that they live in the sense that the writer's words make the reader believe in them absolutely.

Such figures are the parents of the boy, Jannie (Uys himself); Mrs. Kotze, with her "white forehead and long yellow hair" (his

mother, then a delicately made, beautiful young woman, now a
writer herself under the pseudonym of "Sannie Uys"); and Japie
Kotze, the taciturn father who is really Japie Krige, Uys's father
and the famous Springbok rugby player, said in his recent obitu-
ary to be the best three-quarter that ever had been or ever would
be. Another such figure is Nurse Leppan, here given her own
name, whose eccentric appearance and behavior are brilliantly
described. The reader is made to laugh at her and yet to understand why she was so universally beloved and respected.

Other characters from Old Stellenbosch who are spoken of by
their own names are the old Hollander, whom all children feared
for his strangeness and ferocity; the Dutch Reformed Church sex-
ton with the ridiculously appropriate name of Mynheer van Kerkhof ("of the Churchyard")—a man possibly more humane at
times than the children thought, but possibly only drunk then;
and the venerable Professor de Vos, with his great height and his
long white beard, who preaches the funeral sermon for the baby,
Kleinboet, that troubles Jannie so much. The sermon is based on a
text about the death of the child of David and Bathsheba, which
considers only David and ignores the child himself (who, after all,
like Kleinboet, had lost its life without ever having had a chance)
and also Bathsheba (who, after all, had borne the baby in her
body and must have looked white and sad as his mother now
does). These pen portraits have the kind of life that good painted
portraits have. Photographs, on a wall or mantlepiece soon seem
to go dead; but a painting, whenever one looks at it, seems to
move and to express now one aspect of the personality, now another.

The central episode of the dream is excellently handled. There
had been two previous brushes with death in Jannie's experience
—the death of his grandpa, whose funeral he had attended with
solemn respect; and the drowning of his mother's sister, Aunt
Miemie, with her two daughters, Francina and Kathleen—an episode the shock of which to his mother had led to the premature
birth and consequent fatal weakness of Kleinboet. This episode is
movingly described:

They had pieced the story together from the confused accounts of little
three-year-old Fredel who, an hour after the drowning, had been found
wandering about, crying bitterly on the bank of the river. Francina,

who couldn't swim at all, had waded too far out in the pool. Then Kathleen—whom Jannie had taught to do a dog paddle at Onrust the year before—had tried to help her. Aunt Miemie must have just taken off her bathing-costume when her daughters' cries had made her rush to the pool and plunge in after them; for later her clothes as well as her costume were found behind a bush about fifty yards from the river. Two men from the village had dived in and found her there, lying naked at the bottom of the pool, her children clasped in her arms. She must have put up a tremendous struggle for there were deep scratches and bruises on her neck and shoulders where the two girls had clutched frantically at her as they drowned.

We are also told:

There was a flower Jannie would always associate with Kathleen, the frail beautiful bluebell. He had never seen a bluebell before and Kathleen and he had set out from the homestead at Bontebokskloof early one morning to look for tortoises, they had wandered up the deep kloof, got some distance from each other, then Kathleen had called to him excitedly, he had run up to her where she sat crouched at the foot of a moss-covered bank looking at something, he had squatted down beside her—and there they were, the bluebells, a whole cluster of them, a deep sky blue, he had never in all his life seen such a beautiful blue, he had never in all his life seen such beautiful flowers, with such soft delicate petals, standing slim and still and very very shy, it seemed, on their slender stems in the windless air. "Bluebells . . ." Kathleen had whispered. "Bluebells . . ." What a beautiful name, Jannie had thought, and how right, how perfectly right; for those tiny curved blooms looked just like bells and if a breeze were to come up now, they would chime softly one against the other. Then he had looked up into Kathleen's face close to his above the cluster of flowers. Behind her the bank, caught by the first sharp ray of sun, flashed with dew—and for the first time Jannie had found the funny reddish-brown freckles above Kathleen's cheekbones attractive and he had become aware, with a warm feeling inside him, of her eyes: how shy they were and how large, how blue, as blue as the bluebells. . . .

Later, in the dream, these two passages are fused—together with the reminiscence of an exquisite silver-tree that Jannie has seen—into an image of death that contains a strange mixture of beauty and horror:

He couldn't sleep, he would never sleep again, Jannie thought as that night he lay in his bed in the back room. Then he was walking alone in the forest at Claremont. And it was still and quiet and dark,

[133]

but he was not afraid, he did not even feel uneasy but happy, a strange still sort of happiness. Then the forest had changed, it was a different forest, it was the whole world, a strange new world that he alone inhabited. But he did not feel lonely, he had no thoughts, no feelings— only a deep peace and calm. Suddenly everything in the forest was bathed in a thin blue-white light, there was no forest, only a dim sphere like a huge indistinct ball with him, Jannie, at its centre and that vague light hanging like a mist about him.

Then he was standing outside the ball, peering into it, trying to make out what lay behind that pale mist. Soon that shapelessness had solidified, become hard and glassy; and Jannie saw it was a marble, a gigantic blue-and-white marble like those king marbles he had played with when he was younger. In a second everything inside the marble had softened, floated apart, come together again and now there was a snow-white circle round a deep blue core like an eye's iris. All at once Jannie realised it was Kathleen's eye—wide open, unblinking, with a sad, faraway expression in it.

In a second all had changed again, the forest was back: an enormous square block of black crystal with at its centre a slim silver tree that did not glitter or sparkle in the ordinary way but whose light came to Jannie in slow blurred undulations as through water. And now he was walking through that forest, it was a mass of cold black glassy water shifting slowly backwards and forwards. He wanted to get to the silver tree but couldn't, it kept falling back from him. At times it seemed as if the heavy weight of waters had submerged its pale distant glow but then it would be there again like a far faint phosphorescence in the pitch black depths. . . . When Jannie looked up again that silver dazzle was gone and in the tree's place stood his mother, caught in a circle of soft golden light. Bareheaded she stood there, a radiant smile on her face, as calm and golden as the mountain itself. Jannie felt his mother's radiance reaching out to him, but before its warmth could envelop him, he was looking into a dark pool but looking into it as if he stood level with its floor—its waters deadstill as if frozen solid. Then three pale figures came floating, as if from nowhere, into the pool . . . they hung there motionless as though caught in the crystal-clear water, very distinct against the blackness about them. A woman with a girl on either side of her, all three facing Jannie . . . white and still and naked. The glow from their bodies was reflected in three pale circles of light on the ground below their feet. And as the bodies stirred in the current, the circles moved too—revealing, on the pool's dark floor, a pink or softly gleaming starfish.

Presently he sees a fourth body, that of Kleinboet, his dead baby brother and here the horror of death is all concentrated into the vision of the crab: "Kleinboet had turned and on his bare back, close to his short little neck, Jannie saw a big red crab with its two protruding eyes staring malignantly at him and its claws stuck deep into Kleinboet's soft flesh." And the horror of death as expressed in this crab makes itself felt again as Jannie watches the funeral of his baby brother:

It did not take the two men long to lower the coffin into the grave. First his father, then Professor De Vos and then Mynheer van Kerkhof dropped a handful of earth into the grave. Jannie bent down, closed his hand over some earth on top of the mound at his feet, touched with his finger a stone concealed there, moved his hand to the right and, taking a fresh handful, straightened up. The dove was no longer cooing. Stepping forward, he leant over the grave and, stretching out his hand, let the yellow earth trickle through his fingers. He could see the coffin clearly, blacker than the dark earth, at the bottom of the grave. And suddenly he saw Oupa and Kleinboet together in that small coffin, Kleinboet lying on Oupa's chest, his tiny head resting in Oupa's long white beard—and, a second later, the red crab of his nightmare. Then the old stillness had leapt from the grave, that nameless horror was again upon him.

Sick with nausea and with his mind a chaos of whirling images—from which emerged only the distorted faces of Oupa, Tant Miemie, Kathleen, Francina and Kleinboet—Jannie stood swaying on the edge of Kleinboet's grave. The next moment he felt Mynheer van Kerkhof's hand in his, warmth and strength seemed to flow into him from that firm clasp and Jannie had steadied himself. Slowly disengaging his hand, he stepped back amongst the others.

But morbid or even very sorrowful thoughts cannot dominate many normal lives for long. "Cheerfulness keeps breaking in." Jannie, in any case, is the kind of child in whom the life of the body predominates most of the time. Consider, for example, his thoughts on the game of "Kick and Jump," as he wends his reflective way home from the station after spending a couple of weeks in Claremont—these were his thoughts perhaps at the very minute, as he realizes on his arrival home, of the death of Kleinboet from meningitis:

Coming out into the main street, he could still hear his mates laughing and shouting in the far corner of the Braak. It was a good game, Jump-and-Kick, if it hadn't been for Ike Levinson all the boys would have said he was the best Kick-and-Jumper in the whole school. A fine game, a splendid game. He would teach Kleinboet to play it when he was older. And he'd teach him to play it well, as well as he did. And he'd warn him against certain things—not to take too long a run, like Ike Levinson, for instance. Your run shouldn't be too short either. For then you wouldn't get far enough into the air. And you should kick just at the right moment. If you kicked too soon you wouldn't clear the boy, you'd collapse on top of him—and it would be your turn to be kicked. And if you waited too long, you'd kick into thin air as you went sailing over . . . and that, too, would make you the next one to pay for the laughter. The moment to kick was the split second after your hands had touched the middle of the boy's back. A neat quick flick with the right foot downwards and sideways and it would land square on the boy's bottom so that he lurched forward and often fell flat on his face to the amusement of everyone, except, of course, the boy himself. A kick like that, as clean as a whistle, as only he could give it! He'd train Kleinboet, see to it that he ran right, jumped right, kicked right. . . .

And the story ends with Jannie's being sent by Nurse Leppan to put flowers on Kleinboet's grave. He cannot endure the idea, he tries to get out of it, but Nurse Leppan makes him go. When he gets there:

His hands were still trembling when he found in a corner against the railings beneath some withered flowers a tin for the gardenias. It was a yellow-and-green golden syrup tin that glittered at its edges as Jannie lifted it to the sun. There was a lion painted on it with a swarm of bees hovering over the lion and above the bees the inscription: "Out of strength came forth sweetness." Nearby stood a tap and soon Jannie had washed the tin, half filled it with water and arranged the gardenias neatly in it.

Carefully he placed the tin in the middle of the grave just above the spot where he knew Kleinboet was lying. The gardenias looked even more beautiful now, firmer, stronger . . . as if carved out of pure white marble. Jannie could just see the body of the lion with the point of a curved leaf touching its mane. All at once Nurse Leppan was very close to Jannie. She, too, was strong and very very fierce—but out of her sometimes sweetness came.

But he is a little boy and he is a human being—Krige makes us feel both these aspects of him with absolute conviction; and because of this:

He did not use his brakes as he came to the bottom of the hill but took the corner in grand style, swerving in a wide half circle right across the road and narrowly missing a cart coming in the opposite direction. Bending low over the handlebars, he pedalled furiously in order to dive into the dip this side of the bridge at his highest possible speed. As he rose out of the dip like a swallow, the breeze smacked him full in the face, there was a surge of joy within him and his exhilaration seemed to take him by the throat.

CHAPTER 9

Envoy

ONE IS tempted to consider Uys Krige a simple Boer lad and to say that this is what he remains as a writer, despite his middle-age; despite his wanderings through most of the countries of Europe and America; despite his translations of English, French, Spanish and Brazilian poetry; despite his friendships with many living poets of international repute—perhaps even in spite of the complexities of his mind and his often very delicate artistry.

There is some truth in this estimate, for Krige remains a lad in the freshness of his apprehensions and in the warmth of his feelings. He remains a Boer lad because he is impregnated to the marrow of his bones with the education he got from the life described in "The Coffin" and "The Dream"—a kind of life that accords well with another kind which he got to know later on in one of the tensest periods of his life—that of the Partisan peasants whom he portrays in *The Way Out* and in "The Charcoal Burners."

Krige remains simple in that he belongs to that part of civilization that adheres to a belief in what plainly works for the good of humanity: ordinary kindness, ordinary honesty, ordinary courage —one that does not get itself tied up in the one-upmanship that is the disease of parts of older civilizations. This belief also does not stew in self-consciousness, in self-mockery, in cynicism, and in the kind of sterile self-analysis that Lawrence dissects with such mordant insight in his poem "Abysmal Immortality."

Of course, this kind of simplicity has its own dangers, and to these Uys Krige has sometimes yielded, but hardly ever in his later work. Some of his early poems and plays draw morals where none are needed; some neither penetrate very deeply nor consider sufficiently the involvements in what they do penetrate. Very occasionally an early poem or play or story—but very rarely a later one—slants in some political attitude that assesses all too crudely (whether openly or by implication) the difficulties that men are

always having to solve in South Africa. The slant is always in favor of the underdog. Before the Boers got thoroughly into power
in South Africa, it was pro-Boer, as in *Die Arrestasie* and *Die Wit
Muur;* in both, the triumph of the "noble" side seems a shade too
easy. Later, after the Nationalist party in South Africa had alien-
ated almost all non-Nazis, it is pro-African and pro-Colored: "The
Death of a Zulu," "The Two Daumiers," and one or two of the
Groot Begeer poems contain a slightly too easy satire on the folly
and injustice of the white man. One may share Uys Krige's sympa-
thies in both cases, but particularly in "South Africa, renowned
both far and wide/For politics, and little else beside." [1] In this
country a work of literature with a discernible political slant in-
stantly wins applause from at least one group of citizens—and this
very fact spells danger: the issues are so easy to oversimplify.
However, this fault is rare in Krige's work: it is as human beings,
not as political figures, that most of the Colored people of *Ballade
van die Groot Begeer* win sympathy; for it is with what seems permanent in human nature that Krige mainly concerns himself.

But in regarding Uys Krige as nothing more than a simple Boer
lad, one would underestimate him. It is true that he is a poet born
not made, but his artistry, as I hope I have shown in the preceding chapters, is not only exceptionally rich but is "sophisticated" in
the truest sense of that much misused word. For all its appearance
of spontaneity, Krige's work is most carefully written and rewritten; it is often revised and re-revised over a period of many years.

The simple kindness and honesty of heart at the very center of
his writing make it radiate a light and warmth that belong to the
author's own temperament—spontaneous, sociable, optimistic,
generous, responsive. His work is rich in humor, fancy, and inven-
tion; and it is delightful to find as one goes through it chronologi-
cally, that it gets better and better—not only in artistry but in the
solidity and breadth of the basic qualities. *Ballade van die Groot
Begeer* is signally the best of his volumes of poetry; *Die Ryk Weduwee* and *Die Goue Kring* are far and away the best of his plays;
and the tales in *The Dream and the Desert* are much the finest of
his short stories. His strength waxes, and his weaknesses wane as
he gets older.

The artistry grows too, the command of language, rhythm, and
construction. About rhythm and construction enough has been
said in the preceding pages, but perhaps not enough about Krige's

use of the Afrikaans language. He has done his mother tongue a service by helping to free it from the swaddling clothes in which the careful nurses of its comparative infancy had wrapped it. Linguistic purism—fear of Anglicisms and Batavisms, unAfrikaansisms of every kind (a necessary fear, no doubt, at one time)—was tending to impoverish and stultify the language when Krige burst the bonds. He seems a kind of very minor Spenser of the Afrikaans tongue: he combines the racy with the learned and uses new inflections as he chooses. For example, if, for his meter, he needs a longer word than "lid" (limb), he makes a new singular "ledemaat" from the plural "ledemate" and uses that. Or he will say "bronne" for "bron" (source). This kind of thing corresponds with Spenser's use of such words as "hardihead" or "hardiment" when he chooses them instead of "hardiness." In *Die Grote Kanonne* Krige makes his elated characters drop into that very stately sounding language to the ear of an Afrikaner, High Dutch, with comic effect: "Je hebt't gehad" for the slangy English "You've had it," or "Hetgeen gy eens zag," archaic High Dutch for "what you once saw." His characters use a great variety of words and images for "drunk," "geswael" (sulphured); for "strong drink," for example, " 'lawaaiwatertjies" (little waters of noise); such half-mocking images as "ystervreter" (iron-eater) for "frontline soldier"; or such contemptuous ones as "twee hierjy's" (two here, you's) for two nonentities. Or they mix up English with their Afrikaans, assimilating it as people do in conversation as in "ons is nou moubaail" (we are now mobile, mobile being merely spelt in the Afrikaans way); or "Jy brêg" (you brag); or "Moenie pênik nie" (don't panic); but to people who have no Afrikaans, these examples mean so little that I shall not multiply them. Suffice it to say that Krige uses the language with an unusually flexible range, selecting and coining with great fertility.

To this service to the language his translations have contributed largely. This book has already considered his translations of French and Spanish poems; and it concludes with a brief mention of his translations of two plays, one the Spanish *Yerma*, by Lorca, which has been published; the other, still unpublished, of Shakespeare's *Twelfth Night*—parts of which Krige has read aloud with his infectious enthusiasm and emphatic marking of rhythm—an emphasis that, strong as it is, increases one's sense of its subtlety.

Yerma is full of excellent imagery of the simpler Lorca kind—

bold, strong, simple, full of color and light. Dealing as it does with
a few elemental feelings, it seems to get its depth of suggestion
from a living and deep tradition that is capable, one feels, of taking into account the modern world. It is charged with vigor as in
the following passage, where a woman is talking about her lively
baby: "Hy't gebulk soos 'n bulletjie, geskree met die krag van 'n
duisend boomsingertjies wat almal saamsing. En hy't ons nat
gemaak en ons hare getrek, en toe hy vier maande oud is, het hy
ons gesigte van bo tot onder stukkend gekrap." This statement is
full of joy: "He bellowed like a little bull, he screamed with the
power of a thousand cicadas all singing together. And he wet us
and pulled our hair, and when he was four months old he
scratched our faces to pieces from top to bottom." Or as in this
song for the woman who is barren: "Laat bloei die roos, laat bloei
die roos/In die verwelkte skoot." ("Let the rose flower, let the rose
flower/In the withered lap"). Or this lament:

> Helaas vir die vrou
> Dor soos brakland
> Helaas vir die vrou
> Met haar borste van sand

(Alas for the woman/Barren as brackish land/Alas for the
woman/With her breasts of sand.)
  Or one finds images like this from a pregnant woman speaking
of the child inside her: "Het jy nog nooit 'n lewende voëltjie in jou
hand hou vas nie?" (Have you never held a live bird in your
hand?). Or this image of joy and renewal "Skud, takke van die
helder son/Dans, fonteine en elke bron" (Shake, branches in the
clear sun/Dance fountains and every spring).
  I cannot, of course, by translating into English Uys Krige's
translations into Afrikaans, give much idea of their quality; but I
can perhaps give a slight idea of the economy and force with
which this beautiful pastoral play, which is full of the tinkle of
sheep-bells as the flocks go by and of the sound of shells being
blown as a summons on the farms, has taught him.
  Of his *Twaalfde Nag* (Twelfth Night) I shall say only that it
has made me believe (as I did not before) that a good translation
of Shakespeare can have some value even for people who can read
the original in English (as almost anybody can who can understand Shakespeare at all in South Africa). One cannot fail to de-

light in Krige's poetic tact and balance and resourcefulness with which the whole has been done—the rhythms and images of the "poetic" speeches. Their very tone is caught and held, from the dreamy, romantic sentimentality of Orsino to the conviction, humor, and profundity with which Viola speaks to him disguisedly about her own passion—or the reality that breaks into Olivia's language when she rouses from her artificial mourning for her brother. The puns are usually on different words from those in Shakespeare but have a similar effect; they are topical and South African in a way, but they give the Elizabethan sense of language. Moreover, they seem to be played with by the keen witted; words hit flying through the air and hit flying back again with the athletic speed of intelligence and gusto. Then too Sir Andrew's exquisite foolishness, for example, and Malvolio's "naargeestige swartrokkigheid" ("mean-spirited black-frockcoatedness," to borrow a phrase from Eberhardt Planje)—both are reflected in a precise, full, natural Afrikaans which ranges easily from the most stately and formal language to the most colloquial and easy.

The whole translation is a considerable achievement which draws attention to the qualities in Shakespeare's English and to what he is saying rather than distracts people from Shakespeare. It has also added to the resources of Afrikaans by its being used memorably and with so much variety. In English, too, Krige's sensitive ear for language has been sharpened with the years; but he has not yet mastered the niceties of dialogue as he has in Afrikaans. The first edition of *The Way Out* was full of clichés; for, having been imprisoned for years with his English comrades-in-arms, he took the phrases always in their mouths for "good English." Later, discovering his mistake, he spent many months laboriously eliminating the clichés, and so taught himself to write the pure, precise English of *The Dream and the Desert*, where a very occasional use of South African language does not mar but, rather, gives the language it's local flavor.

But Krige remains first and foremost an Afrikaans writer; and the time will come, if the world does not fall to pieces, when he will gain the nationwide recognition that his natural modesty and unassuming temper have prevented—for only the pompous are taken for men of weight. Krige will then be acknowledged as one of the most important writers that Afrikaans has produced—and as one in the foremost ranks of the best.

Uys Krige and Afrikaans

We have thought it both useful and interesting to quote an extract from a lecture delivered by Uys Krige at a literary conference held in Johannesburg in July, 1956. It not only gives a lively idea of the expressiveness of Afrikaans, but provides an original aperçu into what might be called a poet's workshop.

The Afrikaans language was born on the veld. It is as characteristic of our country as the long yellow grasses are characteristic of most of South Africa in winter, or the red earth typical of the Transvaal. And it has the Dutch language which is centuries old as a background or framework. Dutchmen sometimes speak of Afrikaans as "baby talk" when first they hear it or see it in print. But we know what their greatest poets and philologists have thought and said of it once they got acquainted with it. I like Alan Paton's description of it in the *New York Times*: "streamlined Dutch." Though one shouldn't compare languages—each has its own inherent right, its own intrinsic beauties, there is really no such thing as a beautiful or an ugly language—I myself have always seen Afrikaans when flanked by Dutch as a swift highly-manoeuvrable little Spitfire beside a large heavy bomber.

A writer could not wish for a language at a more interesting stage than Afrikaans is to-day. First there is its *taalskeppende vermoë*, its language creating capacity. One finds it everywhere—whether you chat with a Namaqualand farmer, a Hermanus fisherman or a Coloured shepherd on top of the Pakhuis or even a skolly boy of Cape Town's District Six—this terse, vivid, racy, richly idiomatic language which he who speaks it seems to be able to add to (and so enrich) at will. Often the poorest or the most ignorant and backward speak the language at its best. Since their speech has not yet been standardized for them by radio, book or cinema, they are free to create their own language, even their own images, and invent their own idiom out of their own immediate need from their own immediate surroundings.

Let me give you a few examples. And I can give you hundreds. The Hawston fisherman who said to me as the first roll of thunder was heard among the turbulent clouds: *Ja, Basie, die weer is loskop*. It is a magnificent image, both visual and auditory: The weather is loose-head —that is to say, like a horse tossing his mane, rearing up on his hind legs and neighing at the same time. This image, contained in a single adjective, of the oncoming storm as a huge horse on the horizon, is particularly apt when one remembers that in bad weather horses become restive or nervous.

Die weer maak uier: The weather makes udder. One sees very clearly here, the swelling clouds like cows with full udders. And the image, in comparing water, one prime necessity of life (especially in South Africa!), with another of life's prime necessities, milk, not only suggests plentitude, abundance, fecundity and so also joy, but has an added richness because of its humour.

Recently I was discussing with some Coloured students of Battiswood College, Cape Town, a point I had made during the course of a talk given to them on the short story: namely, the very expressive language, its wealth of idiom, humour, etc., our Coloured people have at their command. Within a few seconds I was given half a dozen words or expressions for "illegitimate child": *voorkind; loskind; speelkind; kind wat oor die muur geklouter het; kind wat deur die draad gekruip het;* and, best of all, *Saterdagaand se kind* [1]—an idiom which is funny and sad at the same time, and which I recommend to the special attention of our social reformers.

Take, for instance, the Afrikaans name for a certain Cape fish, *galjoen*. It is a homely word that I have heard on the lips of simple fishing folk since chlidhood. Yet what a proud lineage this ordinary word has, what splendid associations are called to mind by this image of a stately ship cutting, with full spread of sail, the waters! There is the Dutch *galjoen* (ship) and the English *galleon* both derived, I should imagine, from the Spanish *galeon* or the French *galion* (*galee* in fifteenth century French), stemming from the Middle Latin *galea*. And all of them finding their origin in a Greek word I can't pronounce, meaning shark, which was the name for the very first warship in man's maritime history. The galjoen is a fish found only in Cape waters. The word (meaning fish) is not included in the great standard Dutch dictionary of van Dale. So the wheel (or our little galjoen) has come full circle—from the classic shark to the agile greyish-black fish of our own day—and we have been re-instated in our Mediterranean heritage of more than 2,000 years. And by whom? A rough soldier or sailor in the employ of the Dutch East India Company? Or a Coloured fisherman who could neither read nor write?

And what about the name *daeraad* or *dageraad* (dawn) for our rose-coloured fish with the blue and gold scales? With its long mysterious vowels suggesting depth, distance, light, freedom and a far horizon, *daeraad* is a lovely word for a lovely fish. This fish, also, is only found along our coast from Hermanus to Port Elizabeth—so this word, too, was probably coined by a simple fisherman. And the fish has several other names: *magistraat; juds* (judge, because of the red robe judges wear); *daggerhead*—which is, of course, a corruption of *dageraad,* but what a corruption! this new South African English word suggesting both the speed of the fish, how it flashes dagger-like through the white foam, and its brilliance, its colour, blood welling up around a daggerhead after the stabbing upward stroke, etc.; and, last but not least, *college boy,* which is a reference to the typically South African passion for brightly coloured blazers.

So we have six South African words—three Afrikaans and three English ones, just right, *ex unitate vires*—for one little fish, not a bad tally!

And what anonymous fisherman, I wonder, had the pleasant fancy of calling that other dark and attractive little Cape fish with the large lustrous eyes by the charming name, *Frans Madam?* [2] It certainly is a monument to his sense of humour.

I know one word in English for the small insect that here in our country seems the very voice of the sun itself, blowing ceaselessly the sun's vibrant little trumpet, the cicada. My investigations to date have given me half a dozen names in Afrikaans for the cicada. Of course the word cicada or *cigale* in French or *cigarra* in Spanish or *cicala* in Italian has a most evocative Mediterranean association for the European ear. But what sharp visual images the different Afrikaans variations conjure up in our minds!

1. *Boomsingertjie,* the little tree singer. The whole tree, it seems, is singing with light.
2. *Doringbesie*—*besie* meaning "little beast"—the inevitable thorn tree and its inevitable poet.
3. *Waterbesie,* or the strident little voice clamouring in a desiccated bush beside a parched riverbed for the water that is not there or exulting because it is there and so the very voice of the water.
4. *Sonroepertjie,* he who calls upon the sun.
5. *Sonnebesie,* the little animal or beast of the sun. And when I have heard millions of cicadas going at it full tilt at high noon on a scorching midsummer's day I have sometimes transposed the image, I have seen the sun as a gigantic *sonnebees,* a huge beast bellowing from the burning skies. Again, how the Afrikaans for the lady bird, *Onse Lieweheersbesie,* the little animal of our dear Lord, links us with our European heritage and reestablishes us in our common Catholic past. *Besie* is, of course, already familiar,

intimate, implying a certain kindness and trust in the person employing the word . . . much more so than "little animal." But when used in this connection the word at once acquires overtones of a Franciscan intimacy and gentleness. What ancient Dutch or Flemish myth or legend is enshrined in this image of only two words, I do not know. But I'll find out one day . . .

So every trip of mine into the Platteland becomes a writer's thrill, a linguistic adventure. Sometimes I have to take a grab at my box of fifty cigarettes to keep pace with what is going on and start jotting down scraps of the dialogue I am listening to with a stub of pencil. And when the farmer stops dead in his conversational tracks, I just say: *"Toe maar, Oom,* it's nothing, go on . . . don't let me interrupt you." Recently I came back from a four day's stay in Namaqualand with forty expressions, words, idioms I had never heard before. I think the critics of my English writings will concede that I know Afrikaans better than I know English. Yet I rarely hear an English idiom, expression or word that I don't know.

Notes and References

Chapter One

1. Pronunciation of "Uys Krige" in International Phonetic Script: œɪs 'kɣɪχɛ.
2. Olive Schreiner, *Thoughts on South Africa* (London, 1923), p. 247.
3. "Parallel-medium": a term employed in South Africa to designate educational institutions in which the medium of instruction is both official languages.
4. From an unpublished letter in the possession of Professor T. J. Haarhoff.

Chapter Two

1. Uys Krige, *Roy Campbell: A Selection with a Foreword* (Cape Town, 1960), p. 32.

Chapter Three

1. See D. J. Opperman, *Digters van Dertig* (Cape Town, 1953).
2. Uys Krige, *Sout van die Aarde* (Cape Town and Pretoria, 1961), p. 27.

Chapter Four

1. Uys Krige: "Has Africa, Like America, a Characteristic Contribution to Make to Literature?," *Proceedings of a Conference* (Johannesburg, Witwatersrand University Press, 1957), p. 87.
2. *Proceedings*, p. 84.
3. *Proceedings*, p. 82.
4. "La Miseria" in *Die Palmboom* and *The Dream and the Desert*.
5. *Proceedings*, pp. 80, 84.

6. *Contact,* Vol. III, No. 3 (February 6, 1960).

7. He and his wife are divorced; she has remarried and is now living in the Transvaal.

8. With the exception of Professor Rob Antonissen, Afrikaans critics have shown themselves singularly insensitive to the kind of poetry written by Uys Krige.

Chapter Six

1. "Hartebeeshuisie": a simple, very humble little house of wattle and daub.

2. "Beskuit": a kind of rusk.

3. "Lager" or "laager": a fortification of waggons drawn up in a circle with thornbushes in the gaps (Afrikaans: "laër").

4. Emily Dickinson: "Snake."

5. "Bywoner" (literally "by-dweller"); a farm worker who lives on another man's farm, but has his own little house, crops and stock.

6. "Soete inval" (literally: "Sweet fall-in"): the meanings of this expression range—roughly speaking—from "Happy inspiration" to "Welcome."

7. "Mosbolletjie": a kind of bun, flavored with wine must.

Chapter Seven

1. Wordsworth.

2. My translation. Unless otherwise stated, all translations are by me (C.v.H.).

3. "C to C," or "Cape to Cairo" cigarettes, popular in South Africa and the northern desert during the War.

4. "Helderberg": Stellenbosch mountain (lit "Clear mountain").

5. "Liefderik" means something vaguely between "loving," "lovely" and "rich in love."

6. A. E. Housman: "Eight O'clock."

7. "Dagga": an illegal drug, easily grown and much smoked in South Africa, chiefly by the criminal classes. It is, I believe, another name for hashish, or very like it; it is likely if persisted in (one is told) to lead to violence or even madness.

8. I don't wish to be misunderstood; by no means all Colored people live in slums, nor do all white people live out of them. Many Coloreds are well educated, cultured and prosperous, and during my life-time large numbers have risen in the social scale. This progress is now, of course, being thwarted by the Government.

9. "Lion's head": one of the mountains round Cape Town; "Groot Schuur": the "Great Grange," one of the finest examples of Cape-Dutch

architecture, and residence of South African Prime Ministers. Behind it is the statue of Cecil Rhodes, dignified by six monumental lions.

10. Mesembryanthemums.

11. "Merrem": a corruption of "Madam."

Chapter Eight

1. Milton, *Paradise Lost*, Book iv, line 55.

Chapter Nine

1. Roy Campbell.

Appendix

1. Literally: "before-child," "loose-child," "play-child," "child that has scrambled over the wall," "child who has crept through the wire," and "Saturday evening's child."

2. "Frans Madam": "French madam."

Selected Bibliography

I. Primary Sources

1. POETRY   *Kentering.* Pretoria: Van Schaik, 1935.
Rooidag. Pretoria: Van Schaik, 1940.
Oorlogsgedigte. Pretoria: Van Schaik, 1942.
Die Einde van die Pad. Pretoria: Van Schaik, 1947.
Hart Sonder Hawe. Cape Town: Unie-Volkspers, 1949.
Vir die Luit en die Kitaar. Johannesburg: Afrikaanse Pers, 1950.
Ballade van die Groot Begeer. Cape Town: Balkema, 1960.
Gedigte (1927-1940). Pretoria: Van Schaik, 1961.
Éluard en die Surrealisme. Cape Town and Pretoria: Hollands-Afrikaanse Uitgewers Maatskappy (H.A.U.M.), 1962.

2. PLAYS   *Magdalena Retief.* Cape Town: Unie-Volkspers, 1938. (Revised ed. 1948).
Die Wit Muur. Cape Town: Unie-Volkspers, 1940. (Contains "Die Wit Muur," "Die Skaapwagters van Bethlehem," and "Die Arrestasie.")
Alle Paaie Gaan na Rome. Cape Town: Unie-Volkspers, 1949.
Die Twee Lampe. Johannesburg: Afrikaanse Pers, 1951.
Die Sluipskutter. Johannesburg: Afrikaanse Pers, 1951. (Contains "Die Sluipskutter" and "Die Gees van die Water.")
Die Ryk Weduwee. Johannesburg: Afrikaanse Pers, 1953.
Die Goue Kring. Cape Town: Balkema, 1956.
The Sniper. Cape Town and Pretoria: H.A.U.M., 1962.

(Contains "The Arrest," "Fuente Sagrada," "The
Sniper," and "All Roads Lead to Rome.")
The Two Lamps. Cape Town and Pretoria: H.A.U.M.,
1964. (Contains "The Two Lamps" and "The Big
Shots.")

3. PROSE *Die Palmboom.* Pretoria: Van Schaik, 1940.
The Way Out (Italian Intermezzo). London: Collins,
1946. (Revised ed. Cape Town: Maskew Miller,
1955.)
Sol y Sombra. Cape Town: Unie-Volkspers, 1948. (Re-
vised ed., Pretoria: Van Schaik, 1955.)
Ver in die Wêreld. Johannesburg: Afrikaanse Pers, 1951.
The Dream and the Desert. London: Collins, 1953.
Sout van die Aarde. Cape Town and Pretoria: H.A.U.M.,
1961.

4. MISCELLANEOUS *Roy Campbell: A Selection with a Foreword.*
Cape Town: Maskew Miller, 1960.
"Has Africa, Like America, a Characteristic
Contribution to Make to Literature?" *Pro-
ceedings of a Conference.* Johannesburg:
Witwatersrand University Press, 1957.
Incidental and occasional poems, translations,
and articles in such magazines and periodi-
cals as *Huisgenoot, Vandag, Brandwag,
Standpunte, Burger.*

Index

Index

Index